The Team Approach

With Teamwork Anything is Possible

Steven J. Stowell, Ph.D.
Stephanie S. Mead

CMOE Press
Salt Lake City, UT

CMOE, Inc.
9146 South 700 East
Sandy, UT 84070

ISBN # 0-9724627-4-0

First Edition

Editing: Helen Hodgson, Martha Rice, Deb Hedgepeth, Cherissa Newton, and Debbie Stowell
Cover Design: Cohezion
Graphic Design: Design Type Service

This book and other CMOE publications are available by ordering direct from the publisher.

CMOE Press
(801) 569-3444
www.cmoe.com

Acknowledgements

Of course to create a book on teamwork, it takes a team of people working together cohesively—literally a team approach!

- We express our deepest appreciation to our design team, Martha Rice, Deb Hedgepeth, and Cherissa Newton who have played a continuous role in helping us focus and articulate our thoughts in a stimulating way. Each of you provide immeasurable value.

- Thank you to our treasured clients—the source of our inspiration. We are grateful for their trust and willingness to share their time and ideas.

- Our sincerest gratitude goes to the CMOE team for believing in our ideas and serving as a catalyst for our teamwork research and training.

- Special thanks to Helen Hodgson for her editing talents.

- We also wish to thank the CMOE Facilitators and Consultants for their contributions and willingness to share their real teamwork stories and experiences.

- And finally, we couldn't write a book and not acknowledge our families who have supported us during this long and intense process. We hope you all enjoy the finished product!

Special Contributors

The incredibly talented team of CMOE (Center for Management and Organization Effectiveness) Facilitators and Consultants who have contributed stories, examples, and experience to *The Team Approach* are:

- Richard Williams, Ph.D.
- Magella Sergerie
- Bryan Yager
- James Gehrke
- Piper Abodeely
- Marco Chan
- Julie Ziadeh
- Cherissa Newton

Contents

Preface

Spending just a few minutes on the internet or at the library, you will find what appears to be thousands of books on Teamwork. Truly overwhelming, the sheer number indicates that the need to develop high-performance teams is ongoing and that organizations are constantly seeking the methods, tools, and approaches for improving group dynamics. We know you have many choices when it comes to resources on teamwork. So what is really valuable and different about this book, or what has changed since our last book *Teamwork; We Have Met the Enemy and They are Us?*

> The need to develop high-performance teams is ongoing.

First, since our original book on teamwork was published more than 20 years ago, we have been observing and working with many teams in all kinds of organizations. This has provided an enormous opportunity to practice, experiment, and refine our experience, knowledge, and tools. We have learned a lot from some magnificent successes and a few interesting failures in helping teams evolve to the next level.

Second, like all of the products and services produced at CMOE (The Center for Management and Organization Effectiveness), this book is both practical and reader friendly. You can read the book from cover to cover or zoom in on parts that are of high interest to you. We did not write this book to satisfy the curiosity of academicians or theoreticians. It is written for practitioners to use.

Third, the book is built around a model and concepts that are specific and highly applicable to any team. It includes an excellent sampling of things to be used by both team members and team leaders. All of these ideas have been tried and implemented within our own team, at CMOE, as well.

Fourth, we understand that the goal of effective teamwork is not just to eliminate the problems and dysfunction that inevitably arise when a group of people is brought together to achieve a common purpose. We all bring our own unique sets of baggage to the team. There will always be cases of overly competitive individuals, overinflated egos, members who have a thirst for authority, and people who are overly reserved and shy. The real goal of effective teamwork is not to eliminate these human foibles and differences, but rather to create the processes, tools, and skills that allow a team to work with and capitalize on differences and conflicts while managing problems, disruptions, and disappointments.

> **The real goal of effective teamwork is to create the processes, tools, and skills that allow a team to work with and capitalize on differences and conflicts while managing problems, disruptions, and disappointments.**

Fifth, whether your team is a senior leadership team, project team, or simple intact work team; whether you are a team member or team leader; or whether you are building a team or on an existing team, the skills and principles presented here will enable you to unmask the secrets and subtleties of teamwork and achieve extraordinary goals and results.

You will find the central premise presented in this book is very straightforward:

- Teamwork rarely happens by accident. It takes deliberate and conscious effort.

- Teamwork cannot be legislated or mandated by those at the top or in authority. Teamwork has to be owned by its members, with the members taking responsibility for the team's well-being.

- Teamwork is a personal choice or a state of mind. All members must decide where they stand, what they are willing to contribute to the team, and in turn what they will hold back.

- While team development is not a classic, predictable, or controllable science, there are identifiable core building blocks illustrated in the Diamond Model of Teamwork that can be managed and manipulated in useful ways.

- It takes teams of people to collaborate and accomplish truly great things. Whether it is the discovery of the structure of DNA or the construction of the space station, incredible achievements require enormous coordination, cooperation, communication, and esprit de corps. Although individual initiative and talent play a big part, more often than not exceptional results or performance requires collaborative effort and courage.

> **It takes a team of people to collaborate together and accomplish truly great things.**

All of this is not magic; there really is no secret. It can all be put into practice by any team if there is a desire and determination to do so.

We hope you enjoy the reading experience. As always, if you have questions about any of the points in this book, please call us because we enjoy discussing all the different viewpoints of teamwork. Now let's get started...

CHAPTER

ONE

The Will to Team

1

The Will to Team

Teamwork doesn't just happen by chance. Bringing a group of people together to accomplish a task does not guarantee a Mona Lisa-like outcome every time. The construction of a meaningful team requires commitment, resolve, courage, and discipline. Teams are like a splendid building that has been designed and constructed to stand the test of time. It has good architecture and superior engineering behind it. Soil and water analysis has been completed, the climate factored in, quality materials acquired, the best craftsmen assembled, and the schedule laid out before footings can be poured. A sound building requires preparation, investment, and vision.

For those who have built a house or something similar, the process described above is idealistic. Constructing a home, a library, or school never goes according to even the best-laid plan. Construction is never trouble-free because problems inevitably pop up and it usually takes longer than expected. Sub-contractors do not meet their commitments; weather turns bad; or countless small challenges surface. You know what it is like—frustrating. But still, you keep working undaunted because you have a vision and you have faith in the process. You learn to cope and adapt by making the needed adjustments so the architectural plans match the engineering realities. More than likely you will reach a point where you will second guess the whole project and wonder why you ever started it. But you don't turn back.

Things end up better in the long run anyway. Problems get solved, opportunities develop, and solutions emerge.

Constructing a team is very similar. It is not a smooth and perfect process. Like architectural projects, each team will have a different personality, style, and purpose. Some are designed better than others. Some are more efficient; some require a lot of maintenance; while others don't. But they all have unique strengths and, yes, a few flaws. There is no magic bullet or secret formula to constructing a perfect team. It simply requires planning, guidance, discipline, and determination. The hardest part is preparing to turn the first spade of dirt. In other words, making the decision to do it, committing the resources and energy, and taking the first step are the most difficult.

History has taught us that humans discovered the benefits of teamwork early in our evolution. Cave dwellers gathered around campfires to organize hunts, looking out for one another in order to survive. Even species in the animal and insect world have discovered how to work together (or they are genetically hard wired) to improve their existence. Take for instance, the rhino and the oxpeckers, also called tick birds. In Swahili, the tick bird is named "askari wa kifaru," meaning "the rhino's guard." The bird eats the ticks it finds on the rhino and noisily warns of approaching danger. The rhino tolerates the bird's presence, allowing it to feed off the rhino's back.

The principles of teamwork resonate throughout nature as well as human history. It doesn't matter if people are part of an expanding business, a public agency rolling out a new social program, a group of friends organizing a golf tournament, or police officers calling for backup support in a difficult situation, people impact each other in all aspects of their lives. Organizations simply can't function well without the cooperation of their people. When people synchronize their ef-

People who work together are an organization's greatest resource.

forts around common objectives, they can achieve more and do it better, safer, and more efficiently. People who work together are an organization's greatest resource because, as a unit, they can execute tasks, think, manage capital, serve customers, and ensure success.

However, people are people and they make mistakes. People get in each other's way, and at times, fall short on their commitments. Yet, in a team setting they can learn together, develop skills, create relationships, and innovate. This process makes the group more competitive and it helps it survive. Teams also produce concrete rewards that satisfy tangible and intangible personal needs.

Our work with hundreds of groups has revealed at least four issues that can prevent groups from truly functioning as a team:

1. Task fixation (process blindness)

Task fixation causes individual team members to justify any behavior as okay if it contributes to achieving successful completion of the task or goal. Little or no concern is directed to how the group functions as it journeys toward the goal. When a group is fixated on the task, any means justify the ends. In this scenario, individuals tend to focus on their own needs rather than the needs of others. There is a lack of support, valuing of differences, deferring of egos, flexibility, brainstorming, or seeking commitment. Whether subtle or covert, self-centered competition is justified as necessary to achieve the team's target, and in the end the team comes up short.

2. Power struggles

Internal conflicts make up part of the natural dynamics within a team. In less effective teams, there may be battles for leadership, influence, and power. Dominant individuals may scramble to be recognized or influence others in a particular way. Disagreements over ideas are positioned as win-lose alternatives: accepting someone's ideas means rejecting someone else's. Cliques, groups within groups, and "we" versus "them" are terms used to describe this characteristic of ineffective teams. For new teams, this struggle is fostered by the need to find someone who will support your ideas. Once found, the divisiveness of lobbying for a majority vote starts. The "outs" resent the "ins" and resist their ideas, sabotage their plans, or simply refuse to be fully functioning members of the team. It can be an ugly situation and cause the team to fail in its mission.

3. Fight versus flight

The fight-or-flight syndrome occurs most commonly in a team where people are unwilling to listen to each other, fear speaking up, don't trust the team, or the team goal is unclear. Regardless of the behavior, the result is the same: the team loses precious resources, energy, creativity, and collaboration. Decisions are made and plans are implemented with less-than-total group input and support. It is frustrating to be a team member or team leader when this occurs. Unless the team is organizationally mandated to remain intact, this type of dissatisfaction and frustration among the members will cause it to disintegrate.

4. Stereotyping

With this type of team struggle, individual differences are not considered and generalizations about team members' motives and behaviors are made. These stereotypes serve as blinders that keep the group from using all the resources and talents available to the team.

A tight-knit, high-performance team, however, provides its

members with strength and security. When team members feel strong and safe, they can put more energy into creatively solving organizational problems. Without teamwork, people become consumed by destructive politics, in-fighting, and cover-ups, to avoid blame and retribution. The unifying principle of teamwork is pretty simple: together we rise and fall, together we sink or swim, together we laugh or cry. When all is said and done, it is people working together that makes an organization stand out and excel.

"In order to have a winner, the team must have a feeling of unity; every player must put the team first – ahead of personal glory."

– Paul Bear Bryant

Unified teams make adversity more bearable and the good times sweeter. Teams are capable of turning grief into kinship and finding silver linings in calamities. In fact, some research suggests that people who are able to build relationships with others live longer because they are exposed to cooperation, feel safer, and act with confidence and strength. When people band together to help others meet their needs and desires, including personal growth and development, the quality of life improves.

The challenge we face as individuals is whether to contribute positively to our teams or engage in self-centered actions and attitudes. Consciously or unconsciously, these decisions have a huge influence over how team members make each other feel. This is why achieving a high level of teamwork is no accident.

Teams have to be designed and developed correctly and then continuously maintained. The relationship between individual members and the team itself is very symbiotic because those around us can provide positive vibes or they can create a negative environment by quibbling, complaining, sparking rumors, and not speaking up, thereby making life difficult for everyone on the team. People need support to help meet each other's emotional and performance needs.

When it comes to developing teams, there are two schools of thought or two competing forces. It is like the proverbial yin and yang. Some believe that as a species people are drawn to one another, are eager to connect, and are instinctively driven to come together and form groups and communities. This school of thought contends that people want ties to others and want to share mutual benefits. The other school of thought suggests that people are inherently independent, individualistic, self-reliant, and value individual achievement. In other words, people are competitive and aggressive. We contend that if pride, competitiveness, and greed can be overcome the real benefits of teams can be reaped when things are going well, but just as important, teams have a solid foundation to rely on in times of adversity, risk, or when moving to the next level.

Human beings are not destined to be closed, self-regulating systems; rather, they can be open, integrated, and disciplined systems, capable of encouraging, supporting, and orchestrating performance through feedback, communication, and collaboration with co-workers. A connected team is a place where members can encourage, uplift, and promote each other. A team provides an environment that empowers people to maximize their performance.

The path of teamwork can be a long journey that continually evolves. Over our years of working with teams, we have repeatedly said to them, as well to as to our own teams, that the goal of the journey is not to eliminate all problems, conflicts, and challenges, but rather to create an environment where members can resolve problems, manage conflict, and overcome adversity with dignity. The essence of teamwork is achieving goals the team deems desirable. Teamwork is reaching outstanding results while providing a meaningful and enriching experience for all who contribute to the work effort.

Yet, many people talk about teamwork as if it is a no brainer, mistakenly believing that just because a group of smart people gets together, a high-performing team is automatically created.

Teamwork is earned.

It doesn't work like that and it never has. Teamwork is earned. No group of people is automatically entitled to teamwork just because they showed up or because they bring their individual talents to the table.

One of our colleagues, Marco Chan, shared an interesting team experience with us. When he was promoted from Senior Manager of Customer Service to Managing Director of District Operations in a Fortune 500 company, he was faced with several major challenges:

1. He came from outside of the Operations Division, with no personal experience in that type of environment.

2. The district was formed due to the growth of seven other districts in the region. So there was a total of eighteen senior managers who had previously worked for the different districts that typically worked against each other and had their own unique culture.

3. The matrix staff supporting the district was new to the district as well.

Needless to say, after a few months, it became very clear to Marco that there was a need to do something quickly to get the team to work together, overcome the challenges, and help each other if the district was to achieve its goals.

He suggested to the leadership team that they might try to work through the challenges using a workshop approach. Initially, the idea was lukewarm among the team members, but eventually, all the senior managers and the matrix staff agreed to participate in a one week team development experience in the Sawtooth Mountains of Idaho.

To the two facilitators observing the team's behavior, the team was displaying all the signs of a dysfunctional team during the first four days of the experience. On the fourth night, while camping at 7,000 feet above sea level, snow started to fall and began to accumulate around the tents. Then shortly before midnight, one of the senior managers, a big fellow, complained of chest pain and displayed the signs of heart  complications. An emergency call was made, and it was found that the rescue helicopter would not operate until there was sunlight. The only alternative was to catch a boat at a lake about ten miles away, for transport to a hospital to assess his condition.

The team studied the situation thoroughly and figured that they could make it to the lake and get to the hospital before 5:00 a.m. So they decided that they would take that option instead of waiting for the helicopter. With the decision made, the team launched into action to build a stretcher out of material that nature provided. Twelve team members were assigned to carry the stretcher with the ailing team member, and the remainder of the team packed up all the gear and headed down the mountain where they would meet up.

The team with the stretcher made it to the lake in less than three hours and then got to the hospital a little before 5:00 a.m. The medical staff took over and fortunately the ill team member responded very favorably and recovered fully.

The two facilitators seized the opportunity to debrief the incredible team achievement. The team realized that with teamwork they could achieve any goal and overcome any obstacle.

A teamwork creed was created at the end of the debriefing, and it was "The climb to the top, together."

The nine steps to climb to the top were:

Courage: Compromise and give candid feedback (always in the positive).

Dedication: Focus and achieve through 100% participation.

Respect: Listen, accept, and adapt to one another.

Friendship: Support, to talk, to enjoy each other.

Integrity: Maintain at all times and at all costs.

Trust: Freedom to share and depend upon each other.

Empathy: Understand and support.

Compassion: Recognize the needs of others.

Honesty: Complete openness.

In the following two years, the team worked extremely well together, and the performance dramatically improved. The stretcher was mounted in the conference room as a reminder to all of their incredible team experience.

You may have the right people, the resources, and the investment (technology, customers, and marketing programs) to complete your mission. You may also have good policies and organizational infrastructure. All of these things will contribute to good teamwork. But, if you are counting on a combined effort that will produce stellar results, you need something above and beyond the basic ingredients. Solving sticky problems or finding ways to be more competitive, requires effective teamwork. Henry Ford said, "Coming together is a beginning. Keeping together is progress. Working together is success."

The good news is that great teamwork can be accomplished with a regular therapeutic regime. Teamwork doesn't move forward effortlessly, so you may have to step back many times, take an inventory of the team's needs, and plot a course of action. Some people will be afraid of the learning process, afraid of feedback, and/or afraid of change.

We have seen countless teams grow too comfortable with the status quo, become complacent, and develop enormous blind spots to the point that they can't see reality. These unfortunate groups can't or won't see the inefficiencies and discord. At these times it becomes easy to throw in the towel and take what you can get rather than fight for what's right for the organization, customer, and your own vision for the team. If you can get your team on track with a little concerted effort, the benefits will definitely be worth it.

Is it hard? Yes, at times! Will it hurt a little? Sure. Can it be done? Yes! Is it worth it? You bet! Now let's explore how.

CHAPTER
TWO

"I, WE, IT"

2

"I, WE, IT"

On a long business trip to the Middle East, we had an opportunity to reflect on some questions about the human experience. For example, what separates humans from other animal species? Some scientists and experts would point to the size of the human brain. An engineer might suggest that it is the thumb and our ability to manipulate objects skillfully. Those who ascribe to religion would attribute our superiority over other species to divine creation. But whatever your belief is on the subject, human advances over the millennia have been remarkable.

As our plane flew over Asia Minor, we recalled reading about the earliest civilizations that emerged from this part of the world. Some experts claim that the first communities and towns were formed in Asia Minor about 7,000 B.C. We have tried to imagine  what it must have been like as humans discovered how to work together. It must have been challenging as people learned new skills and ways to feed and protect themselves that were fundamentally different from the lifestyle based on hunting, gathering, and following wild herds. Even in the hunt-and-gather stages, members of a hunting party probably plotted how they would take down big game. They undoubtedly had assignments depending on their running speed and accuracy with a spear or bow and arrow. Experience with teamwork truly has its origins in man's early existence, yet we sometimes wonder why it still seems so hard at times to get people to work and play together. Even though evidence has suggested for thousands of years that people can collectively attain strength and achieve security, peace, and sanctuary, people still struggle with many group dysfunctions.

When people decided to stop the nomadic lifestyle and settle down, they began to learn new professions like how to grow crops and domesticate animals. Permanent settlers established walled communities that could work together to improve security and their quality of life. As countless thriving settlements sprang up, people discovered how to mine and smelt ore and work with metal. Again, people experimented with collaborative ventures where they could spread the risks. The first sales and marketing functions emerged as people and communities learned how to trade surplus goods such as grain and pottery, and then later when tools were produced. Clearly, more and more people could see the synergies from cooperation. Cooperation fueled new disciplines that communities needed, like architects, engineers, builders, and healers. Specialization and the division of labor had to be balanced and integrated with this new way of making a livelihood. People were beginning to learn about interdependence and how to blend multiple talents to form a functioning community. Giving up one's fierce independence must have been a difficult choice because a part of all of us yearns to be independent.

As wealth accumulated, money to facilitate trade was created; then accountants and legal experts were needed to trace and manage transactions. Lively trade meant increased travel and transportation. People learned how to create agreements, and with agreements came disputes and conflicts that could either be settled civilly, through an orderly system of procedures, logic, reason, or laws, or through force or even violence. Life became more complicated and even today humans continue to struggle with some pre- and post-historic issues and conflicts.

A famous Renaissance poet, John Donne captured the feel and emotion of what we are trying to say in poem or meditation called "No Man Is An Island." Even though the meaning is somewhat difficult to decipher, it is worth the effort. In this poem, Donne puts forth two essential ideas that underscore teamwork and relationships. The first is that people simply are not isolated from each other. Rather they are interconnected much like the "intersection" we will refer to in this chapter. Secondly, Donne speaks eloquently of our own mortality and the fragility of life. We believe that time is short and that creating the magic of teamwork can't be delayed. Likewise, we have to accept Donne's realization: teams don't last forever. Life is a cycle of conception, birth, development, and termination. A team has cycles too as it is disbanded or some of its members may move on for whatever reason. This can create a feeling of loss. Therefore, each team member shares the responsibility to help the team achieve its potential for as long as it is constituted.

> "One man can be a crucial ingredient on a team, but one man cannot make a team."
> – *Kareem Abdul-Jabbar*

Today, individuals still have to choose whether or not they will combine resources, blend skills, and cooperate. For many, it is a tough choice. Some people learn how to work within and support collective endeavors, and some resist or lack the acumen to contribute effectively in a group setting. Yet, to achieve progress and solve today's problems in business, in the environment, and in politics, people must refine their ability to negotiate, trust, communicate, and connect deeply with other people in order to find solutions to modern problems. It seems odd that we are still threatened by disease pandemics, famine, and violence at unprecedented levels. It makes you wonder if humans can really learn how to collaborate. So in modern times, we still ponder a fundamental question: "Are we better off joining forces with others?" and "Are we better together than we would be if we go it alone as we try to exist?"

In ancient times, as well as in modern times, when groups of people form some type of association three things need to operate in concert. We call these things the "**I**," "**We**," and "**It**."

The "I"

Individuals make a conscious or semi-conscious decision to commit to a group. They decide that more success can be achieved if they contribute their strengths, assets, and resources to a joint endeavor. Teams always work better if this choice is voluntary and not some variation of a forced servitude situation. Along with a group charter is the expectation of each individual that he or she will benefit personally from the association. Even in the earliest teams, there was a "social contract" or informal agreement. People want and expect a tangible or intangible return on their contribution. When it doesn't happen, the team can disintegrate or at a minimum become seriously dysfunctional. It probably happened many times in ancient civilizations, in Greek city states, and in the industrial revolution; and it will happen in the digital age. Conflict and tension will always occur. Personality differences are ever present and teams have to develop the ability to resolve individual differences and integrate their unique tendencies and personalities if the team is to flourish. We call this the "**I**" stage of teamwork, referring to the individual.

> "The basic building block of good teambuilding is for a leader to promote the feeling that every human being is unique and adds value."
>
> – *Unknown*

The "We"

Next, teams of people have to negotiate and define relationships. People have to decide who is going to do what, where, when, and how. It is no small task to reach consensus on how the group will manage its communication and coordi-

"We will surely get to our destination if we join hands." *– Kyi, Aung San*	nate the efforts of many individuals with unique strengths and weaknesses. Consensus takes time, patience, and a unique skill set, in order to be accomplished. Some groups do it well and move on to the next thing, and sometimes groups get mired in

unresolved conflict, spin out of control, fall into atrophy, or revert to a competitive and individually focused group. We call this the "**We**" stage of teamwork, referring to the collective team members.

The "It"

Finally, teams have to navigate through the important tasks required to achieve success: defining the task, developing effective processes and tools, and then executing successfully. We affectionately call this the "**It**". In the "It" phase, people on the team have to again reach agreement on what the target is and how to achieve it (joint strategy). Once again, this phase of group evolution requires agreement and dialogue in order to establish common ground, direction, and shared goals. Doing the "It" well requires collaborative skills to solve problems and make decisions in a way that achieve both synergy and commitment.

To some degree, practicing good teamwork is going to create a certain level of natural tension. The tension centers on doing what is best for the individual (self-interest) vs. doing what is best for the team (community interest). It is important that members of the team resolve this tension. We believe that the needs and interests of individual members can be blended in with the team's needs and interests. However, it is always possible that the group's needs and individual interests can't be successfully resolved. Sometimes, there may be instances where the interests are mutually exclusive or there is a deep and genuine divide or mismatch. In these cases, individuals may have to change or even leave the team and join a group that is more personally aligned and compatible. Keep in mind however; conflict is usually a healthy mechanism that motivates people to search for new and creative ways to mutually satisfy interests.

"I not only use all of the brains I have, but all I can borrow."

– Woodrow Wilson

Clearly all members of a team can't have assignments, opportunities, and rewards exactly when and how they want them. Effective teamwork thrives on flexibility and the adaptability of individual members. To some degree, individual members have to be willing to "surrender" a little, to defer to the needs of the team. We are not talking about ethics, safety, or legal compromises or about pacifying the group, caving in to the majority opinion, or acquiescing to gain acceptance. But we are talking about the ability to accept the team's position on roles, resources, responsibilities, effort, timing, and mission.

This is such a critical point because the magic of teamwork happens when the team and its members intersect. This intersection consists of shared tasks, collective beliefs, valued behaviors, and common goals. When the group can meet at this intersection, it emerges as a powerful entity. It doesn't require that individuals give up their uniqueness, individuality, talents, and dreams. It may just mean some shaping, timing, adjusting, and refining depending on the situation. In some cases, or if the group is struggling, it may simply mean deferring to the leader. The challenge is transferring some of the power from the individuals to the team's center and concentrat-  ing the combined power of the individuals on one focal point. It is a marriage between the "I," "We" and "It." If team members can be flexible and patient as they form the intersection of common values, norms, systems, and beliefs they can create a formidable force to tackle the "It" (challenges, technical problems, or competition in the marketplace). When teams harness raw individual talents and differences and forge effective relationships, they can create enormous strength. The fact is individuals need the team for greater security, strength, purpose, and development. Likewise teams need members who will voluntarily give their full effort—discretionary performance if you will. Teams also need diverse talents, experience, and knowledge if they are to survive and discover better ways to solve problems, create innovative ways to work, and stay razor sharp.

As we have indicated, most people want to be part of something bigger than themselves. Even though we have a desire to be independent, another part of us yearns to join in, contribute, and be part of a unified effort. It can be very exciting and exhilarating. Yet we don't want to permanently sacrifice our uniqueness or totally abandon our personal needs. The inter-section requires a balance; it requires communication, discussion, and negotiation to pull it off. On top of that, teamwork is always in a state of flux with new members coming in and older members going through changes in needs and preferences. The mission of the team will shift from time to time, and the team will face new threats and obstacles. Teams that can intersect the "I," "We," and "It" are truly unstoppable, and their members will become highly motivated, have fun, and build momentum.

The "I," "We," and "It" all came together during the first peak ascent of Mt. Everest. Even though the task called for two men to reach the top, it took a team of 300 people focused on the formidable target. The climb began with 200 men and women hiking supplies to the base camp. Then, 40 highly experienced porters carried supplies to the climbers above the base camp. The best third of the hikers continued up the mountain searching for the optimum pathway and securing the equipment. After the first two-man team had exhausted themselves in climbing as far as they could, they rested while the other two-man team followed their path and then moved ahead, working as far up the mountain as they could go. Using this approach the first pair, Tom Bourdillon and Charles Evans, tried and failed to reach the top, giving the other team, Tenzing Norgay and Edmund Hillary, the chance to reach the summit of Everest. Later, Norgay wrote, "It was only because of the work and sacrifice of all of them that we are now to have our chance at the top."

> **"It was only because of the work and sacrifice of all... that we are now to have our chance at the top."**
> *– Tenzing Norgay*

One major consulting firm discovered that just over 5% of all new businesses are still going after five years. Survival in a competitive environment is never easy. But prosperity can happen if there is collaboration, joint effort, and consensus. Sure, when things are tough and the path is uphill, it can take a toll on people: their patience, morale, and ultimately the rate of success. Like the cogs in a machine, teams need lubrication, maintenance, and occasionally replacement of parts. It doesn't mean the system or team is broken; it just means that the tasks and challenges can wear on people. Like anything else, the team needs to be managed, lead, and maintained over the long haul with its predictable bumps and bruises. If members and leaders are willing to collectively share responsibility for the team, it can succeed. When everyone understands  that teamwork is his or her personal responsibility, alignment, harmony, synchronization, and synergy are the results. When the friction, tension, pressures, and dilemmas are not addressed, examined, and resolved, people become burned out, frustrated, and break down. Teamwork is not an easy ride, but it can produce dramatic benefits if people are fair, patient, and flexible. Clearly it takes discipline, courage, and skill to pause, break down the process, and fix it when you see the signs or hear the squeaks and groans of the team machine that indicate that it is struggling. But diagnosing breakdowns in the challenges of teamwork doesn't require a doctorate in quantum physics. By the same token, teamwork cannot be expected to emerge automatically. The natural human condition suggests that people relish personal achievements, individual recognition, power, and self-determination. So bringing a group of individuals together, where the combined effort exceeds the sum of the individual parts is the focus of the following chapters. In the up-coming chapters, we share many parallels between teamwork and the world all around us, specifically in nature, history, and the animal kingdom. These insights provide a constructive perspective on teamwork.

We will also elaborate and explain the "I," "We," and "It" in more depth and specificity through the Diamond Model of Teamwork. Why a "diamond"? Because a diamond is the most enduring naturally made substance on earth and has exceptional physical qualities. In fact, the word "diamond" stems from the Greek work "adamas," which means invincible. Diamonds are the world's hardest natural material, partly due to the very specific conditions that are required to form a diamond. They are the result of incredible pressures being exerted on the diamonds' core elements. Human teams are also the result of pressures, challenges, and hardships. Diamonds are symbolic of many things, including success, excellence, endurance, commitment, and strength. Rock-solid teamwork can be created if you follow the suggestions and complete the work around each facet of the Diamond Model. We hope you enjoy your learning adventure as we explore the specifics of the "Team Approach."

THE DIAMOND MODEL OF TEAMWORK

THREE

Member:

Teamwork is
Everyone's Responsibility

3

Member:
Teamwork Is
Everyone's Responsibility

Introduction

A friend of ours wanted an adventurous vacation and decided to go to Alaska where she could experience nature with a
sled-dog group. As she shared her experience with us, she made
an interesting observation about the dynamics of sled-dog teams.
When a sled-dog team was about to be harnessed, the dogs

 would bicker and bite and make a
ruckus about who would be har-
nessed up first and who would be in
the lead position. But, when it was
time to move out, they quit biting and put their power struggles
behind them. Each dog applied power, unity, and commitment
to the task, regardless of its position. What is even more interesting is that at the end of the day, despite the infighting that
had taken place, the dogs huddled together to keep warm as
they slept. Each had its own identity, drive, and desires, but when
it came time to deliver performance each dog knew what was
expected and stepped up. Regardless of which dog was chosen
as the leader, all of the dogs needed to be well trained and committed as they combined their efforts toward the common goal.

So the questions are: Are you willing to step up for your
team? Is your team better off because of your membership in

the team? Do you offer distinctive value in some way? In an article in the September/October 1998 issue of *Harvard Business Review,* Peter Drucker said,

> "Every enterprise is composed of people with different skills and knowledge, doing many different kinds of work. For that reason, it must be built on communication, relationships, and individual responsibility. Each member has to think through what he or she aims to accomplish-and make sure that associates know and understand that aim. Each person has to think through what he or she owes to others—and make sure that others understand and approve. Each has to think through what is needed from others—and make sure others know what is expected from them."

Needless to say, without members teams don't exist, and without great team members there won't be a great team effort. At the center of the Diamond Model of Teamwork is the team member because it is the combined effort of members that make up a high-performance team. Whenever an individual accomplishes something spectacular, it is rarely ever done without the support, effort, and commitment of other people. Whether directly or indirectly, there is usually someone else or a group of people working behind the scenes to help support the performance of the member. This book is one example. It is not just us, as authors, that make it a reality. We have an exceptional team of people who have shared experiences and worked hard to convert our ideas into a tangible book that is readable, useful, and hopefully interesting. We are grateful to our team for their selflessness and tremen-

Whenever an individual accomplishes something spectacular, it is rarely ever done without the support, effort, and commitment of other people.

dous talents that, when combined together, result in a great final product.

Over the past two decades there has been an obvious shift in how people participate in their organizations: from a more traditional employee who has basic interpersonal skills and technical abilities, and who obediently follows policies and procedures, to a team member who works in a more empowered, strategic, self-directed, and innovative way. This type of team member must contribute more than just the basic job duties and requirements. He or she must be able to build trust, give feedback to others, make decisions, take risks, handle change, and confront conflict, while fulfilling regular roles and individual responsibilities. The value of having team members who embrace the vision and the possibilities of achieving a high degree of excellence is nearly immeasurable.

"Once we rid ourselves of traditional thinking we can get on with creating the future."

– *James Bertrand*

For a team to achieve its desired results, it takes all team members collectively contributing value and effort. Unfortunately, most teams have had the experience of members who did not reach their highest potential or didn't combine their work with others and the strength of the team is impacted when this happens. Consider the following thought:

There were four people named
Everybody, Somebody, Anybody, and Nobody.

There was an important job to be done and
Everybody was asked to do it.

Everybody was sure Somebody would do it,
Anybody could have done it but Nobody did it.

Somebody got angry about that, because it was
Everybody's job.

Everybody thought Anybody could do it but
Nobody realized that Everybody wouldn't do it.

It ended up that Everybody blamed Somebody
When Nobody did what Anybody could have done.

Author unknown

Of course, there will always be some "bad apples," but this chapter explores how good team members can learn some simple things that will make them great team members.

Some people may be asking, "Why do I need to give more as a team member than I already do? After all, I am doing the basic duties and job requirements, and besides they don't pay me enough as it is." Here is why:

- Effective teams require people with different strengths working together in new ways and at greater speeds.

- Because change is the norm, people need to buy in, extend themselves, and give more of their talent, energy, and intelligence to their teams than in years gone by.

> **"We make a living by what we get. We make a life by what we give."**
> *– Winston Churchill*

- No matter what jobs individuals have, team members have been and will be called on to join with others to make important decisions and tackle critical jobs. They need to know how to communicate ideas, gain support, and create collaborative relationships.

- People find greater professional and personal satisfaction as they participate at higher levels and find the power to make things happen in their team. Albert Einstein said, "Only a life lived for others is a life worthwhile."

- No matter how much we contribute, we as humans have an insatiable appetite for rewards—the grass always looks greener on the other side of the fence. Most people will probably never get paid what they feel they are worth. Don't make compensation the key factor in choosing to be an engaged team member.

Many premier organizations have specific expectations from team members. We have collected expectations and descriptors of team members from a few of our valued clients. As you look through these real examples, you may detect some common themes.

A Telecom Company:

"Team members should actively participate in establishing and promoting a team environment; work closely with other departments as necessary; share due credit with coworkers; support group decisions; and solicit opinions from coworkers."

A Financial Institution:

"A team member should demonstrate a positive regard for others by being readily accessible. Willingly assists other team members with questions, concerns, or problems. Considers the impact of decisions. Shares credit and recognition for accomplishments."

A Consumer Products Company:

"Successful team members work effectively with all types of people in order to pursue the organization's goals. They adjust individual goals in order to focus on group objectives. They seek out ways to support and help other team members. They demonstrate respect for all individuals and value the contribution of others. They are always reliable."

A Pharmaceutical Company:

"Demonstrate the ability and willingness to work well with others. Share resources. Contribute to collective success by willingly collaborating with other team members. Respect others' ideas and opinions."

Isn't it interesting to see so many common characteristics within these very different professions? Although, these themes and characteristics may be familiar to you and your organization, these ideas may give you some solid guidelines if you have ever been unclear about the specific behaviors and qualities it takes to be an effective member of a high performing team. Furthermore, these may be things that you would like to see everyone on your team ascribe to.

Membership Close Up

We often hear the phrase that there is no "I" in teamwork. While grammatically speaking that is true, from a practical perspective, we contend that there is a huge "I" in teamwork. Sometimes it is hard to see, but when you think about it, it makes perfect sense. Teams are composed of individuals; they are the essential building blocks of teams. Because individual actions have an enormous effect on a team's performance and atmosphere, individuals must take responsibility for the quality of the teamwork. So it is the individual who decides whether the team will be functional, dysfunctional, or high performing. We believe individuals have the responsibility and the duty to step up and "pull the teamwork wagon."

> "Great discoveries and improvements invariably involve the cooperation of many minds. I may be given credit for having blazed the trail, but when I look at the subsequent developments I feel the credit is due to others rather than myself."
> – *Alexander Graham Bell*

When we interact, decide, and problem-solve with others, we make a choice to be:

• Angry		• Upbeat
• Withdrawn		• Candid
• Disengaged		• Courageous
• Fearful	*Or*	• Cooperative
• Bitter		• Trustworthy
• Resentful		• Committed
• Vengeful		• Understanding

Deciding to be a responsible team member is a choice; it is an internal decision we all have to make.

To be an effective team member you first have to be a decent human being. You need the same qualities as a good citizen or a good Boy or Girl Scout. We call these attributes the **"Fundamental Qualities"** of membership. These core qualities are prerequisites to "play the game." In a team setting, this first group of qualities is non-negotiable.

The second group of qualities is needed in order for the team to just be operational. They are called the **"Primary Qualities."** If a team is to be functional and reasonably effective, you need people to excel in these qualities.

The third and final group of qualities is called the **"Secondary Qualities"** because people need to have these qualities in order to achieve a sustained level of high performance rather than being capable of excelling only when a crisis develops, when people have no choice but to rally together.

Work groups can usually find people with the Fundamental Qualities needed for a team to survive, but teams have to do more in order to elevate, excel, and thrive long term. This requires that members choose to develop qualities in both the Primary and Secondary levels. If a team is to ever achieve economic stability, profitability, efficiency, service, quality, and innovation, it will be the result of individuals stepping up personally and collectively in order to contribute and compete in a global arena.

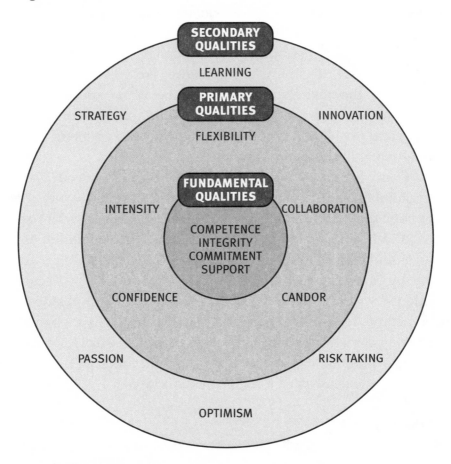

FUNDAMENTAL QUALITIES
Competence

Competent team members have the technical expertise to do their jobs proficiently. Being competent is the price of entry to the team; everyone on the team needs to have a skill, capability, or talent that he or she can offer the team. To build respect and credibility you have to be proficient at some discipline. Competence in a core skill area is one of the foundational elements of team membership and some people believe that proficiency in that area is all that is required by the organization. For us, nothing could be further from the truth: compe- tence or knowledge is just the starting point of team membership. Teams need to be cautious about the false sense of security that can develop from excessive "technical" competence. We will refer to it in the next chapter as the "curse of the brilliant." In other words, you need a healthy measure of common sense and some social and emotional intelligence to go along with finely tuned professional abilities.

Competent team members are achievement oriented. They master their skills and utilize their experience. They work hard to hone their skills. Being open to learning is an important attribute of competent team members. They search out unknown areas and take on challenging endeavors. Michael J. Gelb said, ". . . by stretching yourself beyond your perceived level of confidence you accelerate your development of competence." Sometimes to be fully competent, people have to pay their dues or bring something to the table. But competence has to be balanced with good judgment: doing the right things at the right time for the team as well as for the individual.

Integrity

Team members with integrity are truthful, keep private information confidential, and can be trusted. They don't seek personal gain at the expense of others; they promote fairness and quality within the team, and they keep confidences.

> "If you have integrity, nothing else matters. If you don't have integrity, nothing else matters."
>
> – *Alan Simpson*

Team members who function with integrity know what is right and what is wrong, and they choose to do the right thing, without having to think about it. They know what is fair, legal, and ethical;

when they are in a questionable situation, there is no mental debate. These team members have a strong set of values and a moral compass. Their behavior isn't complicated and it really isn't that controversial. They simply do what they say they will do; they don't misrepresent the truth. They speak with honesty and sincerity, and they don't tell partial truths, exaggerate the truth, or spin it to achieve self-interest.

People with integrity treat the team's material resources as if they were their own. They don't engage in activities during the work day that are not part of the job. A person with integrity can't cheat a customer, a coworker, or the owners. It just isn't part of their nature to distort, fabricate, mislead, or stretch the facts.

Another bedrock quality of integrity is trustworthiness. This stems from a pattern of follow through. Trustworthy team members keep agreements. They can be counted on. They do what is asked of them or they are not afraid to seek out help if they get in a bind. The following poem characterizes this type of team member:

> **"You have to be honest with people. You have to have great respect for yourself. If you see something that is not right, you must do something about it."**
>
> *– Annie Wauneka*
> *Freedom Award Winner*

Integrity
By Peter Cajander

No trace of selfishness,
No doubt,
No fear.

No one to blame,
Nothing to gain,
Nothing to lose.

Standing firm,
Upright,
With straight pose,
Clear eyes,
And a pure mind.

Heart of gold,
Courage of a bold,
Always humble,
Never stumbles,
Firm in action.

No hesitation,
No doubt,
No fear.
Strong actions,
Beautiful moves,
Kind eyes,
And most of all,
Outspoken with deeds.

No excuses,
No bad circumstances,
Consistent,
Reasonable,
Determined.
But still flexible,
Humble,
And sensitive.

Honest to one,
Within,
Always.
Without doubt,

Despising fear,
Often facing
External pressures,
Measures of strength,
Will and courage.

Standing firm,
Upright,
Beauty in the eye,
Courage in the mind,
Determination in the will,
Sealed by golden,
Within.

Commitment

Team members who are committed stay on task, are focused on their roles and doing them above minimum standards. They are not constantly looking for the next big personal opportunistic way to get ahead. We are not saying that they don't have tremendous personal ambition. Ambition and desire are good things for a team. What we are referring to is when people seek advancement at the expense of their current role or team. Committed team members are steadfastly loyal to the team and its mission. They are engaged in their work both mentally and physically every day. Forty-two independent Gallup studies have found that approximately 75% of employees are not engaged with their job. That is astonishing when considering the ramifications disengaged team members have to the bottom line.

> **"Aerodynamically the bumblebee should'nt be able to fly, but the bumblebee doesn't know that so it goes on flying anyway."**
> *– Mary Kay Ash*

Committed team members are clear about their assignments and goals, and they possess the tenacity to stick with a task until it is completed. They know how they fit, and they are aligned with the team goals. These members work hard and play hard. They show up and they never give up. They report back on their progress and keep others informed of what they are doing.

Committed people are true champions for their teams because they address concerns quickly to prevent issues from festering. They are willing to work through difficult relationships.

Committed team members take ownership and act responsibly. They own up to mistakes, are willing to be vulnerable, and are receptive to feedback and advice. Team members don't cover up their mistakes or problems; rather they use them as ways to develop experience and better judgment in future assignments. Responsible team members are accountable for their actions and choices. Committed members don't duck when mistakes or oversights occur. They don't fear questions and they can handle accusations. Their intentions are positive and they don't blame others or excuse away their missteps or misstatements.

> Committed team members not only look out for their own self interests; they also look out for the team as a whole.

Being responsible also means being dependent and reliable. These team members can be counted on regardless of the situation. Committed team members not only look out for their own self-interests; they also look out for the team as a whole. In short, they are willing to put the interests of the team ahead of their own when it is important to do so.

Rudyard Kipling's "Law of the Jungle" has an interesting message about commitment to a team, in this case a pack: there  are times when committing to the rules of the pack or team is more important than self-interests. As a result, the wolf, or team member, will "prosper" because ". . . the strength of the Pack is the Wolf, and the strength of the Wolf is the Pack."

The Law of the Jungle
(From *The Jungle Book*)

Now this is the Law of the Jungle—as old and as true as the sky;
And the Wolf that shall keep it may prosper, but the Wolf that shall break it must die.

As the creeper that girdles the tree-trunk the Law runneth forward and back —
For the strength of the Pack is the Wolf, and the strength of the Wolf is the Pack.

Wash daily from nose-tip to tail-tip; drink deeply, but never too deep;
And remember the night is for hunting, and forget not the day is for sleep.

The Jackal may follow the Tiger, but, Cub, when thy whiskers are grown,
Remember the Wolf is a Hunter-go forth and get food of thine own.

Keep peace with Lords of the Jungle-the Tiger, the Panther, and Bear.
And trouble not Hathi the Silent, and mock not the Boar in his lair.

When Pack meets with Pack in the Jungle, and neither will go from the trail,
Lie down till the leaders have spoken-it may be fair words shall prevail.

When ye fight with a Wolf of the Pack, ye must fight him alone and afar,
Lest others take part in the quarrel, and the Pack be diminished by war.

The Lair of the Wolf is his refuge, and where he has made him his home,
Not even the Head Wolf may enter, not even the Council may come.

The Lair of the Wolf is his refuge, but where he has digged it too plain,
The Council shall send him a message, and so he shall change it again.

If ye kill before midnight, be silent, and wake not the woods with your bay,
Lest ye frighten the deer from the crop, and your brothers go empty away.

Ye may kill for yourselves, and your mates, and your cubs as they need, and ye can;
But kill not for pleasure of killing, and *seven* times *never kill* Man!

If ye plunder his Kill from a weaker, devour not all in thy pride;
Pack-Right is the right of the meanest; so leave him the head and the hide.

The Kill of the Pack is the meat of the Pack. Ye must eat where it lies;
And no one may carry away of that meat to his lair, *or he dies.*

The Kill of the Wolf is the meat of the Wolf. He may do what he will;
But, till he has given permission, the Pack may not eat of that Kill.

Cub-Right is the right of the Yearling. From all of his Pack he may claim
Full-gorge when the killer has eaten; and none may refuse him the same.

Lair-Right is the right of the Mother. From all of her years she may claim
One haunch of each kill for her litter, and none may deny her the same.

Cave-Right is the right of the Father — to hunt by himself for his own:
He is freed of all calls to the Pack; he is judged by the Council alone.
Because of his age and his cunning, because of his grip and his paw,
In all that the Law leaveth open, the word of your Head Wolf is Law.

Now these are the Laws of the Jungle, and many and mighty are they;
But the head and the hoof of the Law and the haunch and the hump is — Obey!

Commitment is a long-term dedication that is strengthened
as team members diligently work to reach new levels of success and as the team faces challenges and adversity.

Commitment is a real litmus test for each member's team-
ing abilities. Unless members see the symbiotic relationship
between the "I" and the "We," the best a team can become is
an okay work group. Committed team members can make personal sacrifices and tradeoffs for the long term health and well-
being of their fellow team members. They subscribe to the notion that in order to add value they must strengthen their shoul-
ders rather than have their load lightened.

Support

Supportive team members genuinely care about and are
protective of other team members. They are available and ready
to help with work and non-work problems. They are empathetic
and compassionate about the trials and challenges of those on
the team who are less fortunate. They are easy to approach
and interact with, so they put others at ease. Supportive team
members are patient and interface well with the style and personalities of others; they build rapport and listen attentively.
Bringing out the best in their colleagues and recognizing their
achievements and contributions are important. Supportive

team members won't gossip, spread rumors, or complain behind the backs of their colleagues. They realize that they have a responsibility to give something back to the team whether it is sharing knowledge and expertise, assisting others with problems or questions, or making a personal sacrifice for the benefit of the team collectively. Supportive team members are able to let go of "old baggage," forgive a little, and move on. They anticipate the needs of others and respond. Because they are fair, respectful, patient, and demonstrate a healthy measure of humility, they are able to sustain long-term relationships.

Supportive team players understand what we call the "reciprocal support equation," which consists of the following:

1. An awareness of when others need some help, plus

2. A willingness to give or offer help in a genuine way, plus

3. The ability and courage to accept help when needed in return.

Millicent Fenwick, a former Congresswoman who was fiercely committed to human rights, said, "The greatest source of happiness is forgetting yourself and trying seriously and honestly to be useful to others."

PRIMARY QUALITIES
Flexibility

One of the most important abilities of a team member, is being flexible and is related to many other qualities. Effective team members are able to change and evolve as the team grows and develops or as its mission evolves. Flexible team members are versatile and can contribute to more than one role when the situation requires an adjustment.

> "Stay committed to your decisions, but stay flexible in your approach."
> – *Tom Robbins*
> *American novelist*

But flexibility goes beyond actions

alone. Flexible team members are open-minded and can be influenced as well as influence. They have the ability to see a broader perspective and to understand the context of the situation. They strive to be objective and recognize when it is appropriate to compromise rather than compete or fight. But these adjustments are not made merely to promote harmony and goodwill; they are made because they are in the best interest of the team collectively.

Team members with limited flexibility can be described as rigid, intolerant, resistant to change, unwilling to change behavior, comfortable with the status quo, and narrow-minded. By contrast, team members with high flexibility tend to be comfortable, willing to explore new ideas, easy to understand, and cooperative.

Collaboration

Collaboration stretches beyond flexibility and compromise. Collaboration is the result of a concentrated effort to find the "win-win" solution. This requires an ability to integrate ideas and weave the creative thinking of two or more people. Collaborative team members actively seek out and include others in key decisions and in creative problem-solving tasks. They share information and they seek assistance when an optimal solution is needed. They seek to understand what others mean, see, or believe, especially when others disagree with their perspective. Collaborative team players understand that conflict and differences, when handled constructively, are the fuel and combustion for creative breakthroughs. This consultative approach helps unite the team in a way that it can produce better results for all of its stakeholders.

The Collaboration Competency and Ability Matrix, utilized by one of our clients, demonstrates that the emphasis needs to be on group efforts to solve problems and not in defending particular individual positions or factions.

COLLABORATION COMPETECY:

Observer	• Recognizes own effective and ineffective behaviors that impact others. • Rarely talks over others during critical conversation.
User	• Contributes to group discussions by challenging and adding valuable ideas. • Demonstrates the capacity to give and take (compromise).
Specialist	• Models skills to create a collaborative atmosphere. • Recognizes and embraces differing points of view. Then facilitates others in discussion and resolution of conflict.
Expert	• Identifies key factors or obstacles that are impeding a group from moving forwards. • Coaches others using a positive and open approach.
Master	• Ensures collaboration skills are a standard way of "doing business." • Models the collaborative process at top levels.

Candor

Candid team members provide the information other team members need to know in order to do the work of the team, solve problems, and make accurate and timely decisions. They can get their message across and have the desired effect. Effective team members present the unvarnished truth in a way that allows people to hear it without feeling attacked or becoming defensive. They can disagree with others without being hostile or cantankerous. They don't communicate with hidden agendas or manipulative influence; rather, they maintain a healthy and open two-way dialogue.

Candid team members are expressive. They speak up and speak out about issues, but they don't dominate discussions with their facts, opinions, or feelings. They look for ways to draw others into the conversation. They confront issues and conflicts openly and give feedback to others in a respectful way. Candid team members "put their cards on the table" and disclose their preferences, insights, beliefs without coming across as belligerent or absolute. In fact they acknowledge that their information and ideas are never perfect and that they have a partial view of reality.

Confidence

Gaining the right amount of confidence can be tricky. On the one hand, we see high-performing teams populated by talented, smart, and confident people, but we also see people with an appropriate amount of humility and a bit self-effacing. Confident team members demonstrate their pride without arrogance-arrogance is a major turn off for other colleagues. When team members have the right amount of confidence, they have self-assurance to take a stand on important or controversial issues. This doesn't mean you need to be stubborn or inflexible. It just means that when your view or position has merit, you will engage, debate, and present your case with poise, confidence, and courage.

Confident team members are able to advocate for their cause or point of view without alienating others. It can be easy for a team member to generate defensiveness and bog down the team after he or she has been heard and his or her ideas have been considered carefully but had them rejected. It can take as much courage to back off a position as it can to argue one. But the key to gaining confidence is to know what is worth fighting for and when to graciously yield to the data, interpretation, or preferences of the collective team. High-performing teams are looking for people who can think on their own and who can be comfortable when conflicts and differences arise. Confident people are change agents; they spark new ways of thinking and doing jobs. They absorb information and will look outside of the box.

Intensity

Have you noticed that when you are around people who can truly execute there is electricity in the air because you know things will happen. Let us be clear: there is a difference between a team member who makes significant contributions and someone who simply shows up and follows instructions faithfully. We are also not referring here to "loose cannons"—people who shoot from the hip and don't think things through.

What we are talking about is someone who knows the meaning of "contribution." These are people who deliver more than what is expected. Effective team members understand when they are in the moment and seize it (carpe diem). They don't need supervision. They do need a good partner, a trusted advisor, or a leader who consults with them. These people can play leadership roles at times because they know when to take action and how to push for results. The key is that intense executors don't let those who move at a more methodical pace or who have modest capabilities irritate them or drive a wedge in the team because these people have energy and are on a mission. They need others on the team who are thinkers and analytical types to help keep them balanced and headed in the right direction. You can count on contributors to handle problems before going to others. These self-starters are very enterprising and fun to be around because good things tend to happen when they are on point.

SECONDARY QUALITIES
Learning

Learners like to discover new skills and develop new talents. They are teachable and willing to be novices. Teams need team members who relish the hard work of learning a new skill or acquiring a new talent. Learners have a level of self-patience and are not too critical of themselves as they make errors along the learning journey. They know that learning demands a price for the lessons; they see this as an investment, or the cost of doing business. When mistakes occur, they see them as successful failures; the result was not optimal but the learning was. Bob, one of the CEOs we have worked with, calls this his personal "continuing education effort." Others look at it as their personal continuous improvement process. In short, learners are change-able; they want to stay current both in the technical arena, and in the social and mental side of their development.

> **Teams need team members who relish the hard work of learning a new skill or acquiring a new talent.**

Learners are aware of their strengths and weaknesses. While they may never turn a weakness into a shining strength, they are willing to plug the gaps and neutralize skill deficiencies so that they are not a drag on their performance. They regularly contemplate, reflect, and evaluate their growth. Learners believe that success means they can never stop learning. Without a thirst for knowledge, atrophy is imminent.

In the book, *Soar with Your Strengths,* Donald O. Clifton and Paula Nelson suggest some simple steps for getting on the right path: "Learn how to stop wasting time worrying about your weaknesses. . . Learn how to double and triple your productivity and effectiveness by exercising your strengths. . . Learn strategies to "manage" the things you don't do well and ways to identify, nurture, and intensify the things you do best."

Innovation

Innovative team members can cope and adjust to changing circumstances. They shift gears easily with new ideas and don't get frustrated when things are unsettled. Their modus operandi is to act on new knowledge by thinking about how it applies to their work and how they can continually add new value to the team. Innovators constantly look for creative ways to tackle overlooked problems. They are inquisitive and curious about everything that goes on in their team and their work. They are always on the lookout for new ways of doing things. They are not afraid to challenge the status quo by asking why, why not, and how come.

Innovative team members are good observers and they will benchmark other professions and teams. They are capable of being different, of standing out and disagreeing without being disagreeable by nature. Their contrarian views do not come across as adversarial nor do they suggest displeasure or feel contempt toward other colleagues. For them it is not "who's" right but rather "what's" right for the situation. The motive behind all of this out-of-the-box thinking is not to "willy-nilly" attack traditions, processes, and rituals in the team, but rather to look for ways that the team can improve their collective performance.

In an interview in *Business Innovation*, Fred Smith of Fed Ex explained his perspective on team-member innovation. He said, "We strive to have a culture where each member of the team feels free to advance good ideas for improvement. The organization must be willing to take calculated risks, rewarding successes, and learning from failures."

Risk taking

Effective risk takers can comfortably handle risk and uncertainty. They use good judgment when taking calculated risks without always "swing-

ing for the fence" (going for a home run) whenever an opportunity comes along. They can also maintain composure when
under pressure.

Risk-taking links to so many other elements of being a high
performing team member. For example, you can't be a candid

> "Progress always
> involves risk. You
> can't steal second
> base and keep your
> feet on first."
>
> – *Frederick Wilcox*

communicator unless you are willing to take
the risk of speaking up. Professor Jerry
Harvey calls it the Abilene Paradox: when
teams take action contrary to their real desires because members won't articulate their
true beliefs, feelings, and intuitions. They
may fear being branded as non-team players, separated from the group or ostracized
because of one's contrarian perspectives. Yet, not speaking out
really is the epitome of being a non-team player because teams
risk taking unnecessary or counter-productive trips "to
Abilene".

Risk taking doesn't mean being wild and crazy with ideas
and actions. What it does mean is being courageous and assertive when you have something to offer. It is having the self-
confidence in your proposals so you can stand up to debate
and scrutiny. It means having the maturity and presence of
mind to adjust and modify your position as others weigh in on
the subject. Collaboration requires risk taking; being an innovator does too. So does having confidence and integrity, and
being a strategist. All of these qualities depend on your willingness to put it on the line.

Optimism

Abraham Lincoln once said, "Most people are as happy as
they make up their minds to be." This notion seems to apply to
team members who truly pull their weight and then some.
Optimistic team members seem to have an innate sense of op-
timism that things will turn out well in the long run. We don't

think they are just being naïve or "overly" optimistic about things. They simply want to be a part of the team; they believe in what the team is doing and believe that the people on the team will succeed together. Optimists realize that to move forward they may have to back up at first or move sideways before they get going. They realize that setbacks and tragedies inevitably happen; but they are not fatalists, nor do they get discouraged. They seem to cope with discouragement without making others around them feel discouraged. Discouragement for them is a temporary thing. They get over it, move on, and rely on their other qualities to pull them through tough times. Even when optimistic team members are not feeling good, they help others feel better. It is not about masking negative moments; rather, it is their ability to put these moments in context, see the bigger picture, and search for the silver lining that may be lurking just out of sight.

> **"One of the things I learned the hard way was that it doesn't pay to get discouraged."**
>
> *– Lucille Ball*

The optimistic team members that we have encountered in our consulting work can accept the things that they cannot change in a positive way. They seem to know how to walk away from negativity, work around it, turn it into a positive, or give it a rest. For them life is short and they have two choices; either they can act like victims and spread negativity to their colleagues or they can tackle their jobs with enthusiasm and choose their emotions. They expect the best will happen and can live with the situation even when the desired outcome doesn't occur.

Passion

Passionate team members enjoy coming to work and genuinely like their jobs. They know what they need to do to help the team operate at peak performance. People who have passion for their work know their part and want to succeed.

In order to be a serious contributor to your team, you need to truly enjoy your work. You need to discover the attraction

> **In order to be a serious contributor to your team, you need to truly enjoy your work.**

and what it is that gives you a sense of joy and fulfillment, then you need to expand on that, tell others about it, and get the team to build more of it into your role. Without discovering the source of your passion, you end up going through rote motions and the job becomes less and less stimulating.

When we say discover we mean just that. A few fortunate people automatically have a "love at first sight" experience with their work. Sometimes, it is easy to lose sight of the passion when less desirable responsibilities and duties are required. Passionate team members find new ways to keep the relationship with their work fresh; they experiment and learn new things as a way of challenging themselves. It doesn't mean that if you are on a surgical team that you willy-nilly experiment on your own during an operation. But it does mean that you do your research, benchmark, and search for better ways to perform. It means you bring new information to your team and continuously improve your skills.

We have one member of our team who has instructed the same class for over 20 years. We asked him how he stays fresh and invigorated with the topic. He said he volunteers to help when the materials are improved. He collects new ideas from each class and lets the participants teach him. He is good, and he has earned the right to try new ideas and experiment in appropriate ways. Some day he says he will write a book about this topic, but in the meantime, he challenges himself to get better all the time.

Strategy

We have actually dedicated a whole book to the topic of personal "work strategy" called, *Ahead of the Curve.* It is based on the notion that everyone on a team needs to be more strategic about their work because you can't get traction for an organization wide strategy if only a few people at the top think and act strategically. Strategy needs not only be to derived from the top down, but also from the bottom up. This is critical because if the organization is to make strategic progress, everyone has to help. A strategic organization is built around strategic people. Strategic team members have a responsibility to be more entrepreneurial and enterprising about their own work. This means figuring out how to be more strategic within their own realm of responsibility, as well as helping add value to the overall strategy. What we have gleaned from our research data is that some team members understand this so well that they can anticipate future eventualities and have a vision for the future. They want to shape the future and not be shaped by it. They tend to have a long view of their job, and they ask themselves strategic questions like, "How will my job change in the future?", "What will my customers need in the future?", "What are the strategic opportunities and threats that I should be thinking about for the future?", and "What do I need to do to keep myself competitive and relevant rather than irrelevant?"

Once again, these qualities link together because a strategist utilizes the learner, innovator, and risk-taker qualities and blends them with the ability to think proactively. Strategic team members anticipate problems before they unfold and seize opportunities when windows open. The performer in them means they don't passively wait for the window to open: they get up, unlock, and lift open windows of opportunity.

> **Strategic team members anticipate problems before they unfold and seize opportnities when windows open.**

As we wrap up our discussion of the role of the member in the Diamond Model of Teamwork, we need to emphasize that in order to sustain success, team players need all of the "Fundamental Qualities"; they also need to excel in at least three of the five "Primary Qualities" and four of the six "Secondary Qualities." Everyone should have a personal action plan to develop and maintain proficiency in the areas that may not be natural strengths. One senior leader we have worked with for many years asked each team member to prepare a personal score card to help track their progress on the qualities we have been presenting.

As with many facets of teamwork, it comes down to your outlook. Effective team membership is essentially a state of mind backed up by consistent actions. It is how you think and feel about your role in the team. Some team members can't or won't reach out to other team members because they are afraid of letting go of their insecurities, vulnerabilities, old habits, and traditions; so they fail to change or to grow into value added members. We witness it on a daily basis: people who focus on the past and harbor animosity or jealousy. We see members who whine or complain about nearly everything, even good changes. We see those who monopolize the limelight, seek approval (the disease to please), and who won't share the credit for achievements. These are people who regularly act like helpless victims and can't move forward or exercise positive influence on a situation. There are also far too many power seekers, attack dogs, and ego maniacs in organizations today.

> "Progress comes from caring more about what needs to be done than about who gets credit."
> *– Dorothy Height*

Yet we have hope when we see people who are a little less competitive with their colleagues or who choose not to take offense, even when mean-spirited comments come their way. Solid team players find it virtually impossible for another person to offend them. Our responses are largely choices we make. Our reactions are not a foregone conclusion, requirement, or innate condition that is imposed on us by someone or something. As rational thinking humans, we can act independently; it doesn't have to be a locked in, cause and effect or an automatic response. We emphasize this point because as team members, we will encounter situations on a routine basis when we could feel bitter, insulted, overlooked, or devalued in some way if we permit it. When we choose to interpret these negative situations as "worst-case scenarios," we give away our personal power and enable others to pull our strings and push our buttons. This is not an invitation to let others walk on you. Quite the opposite, you can be assertive, rather than aggressive, in return as you resolve a dispute. You can establish boundaries and call people out if they are using words, tones, or non-verbal actions that seem intended to hurt you or anyone else on the team. In most cases, people have blind spots, they misspeak, or they are still developing a solid level of sensitivity, or emotional intelligence. Some people unfortunately never get it. Rather than engaging in sophomoric "pay-back" retaliation, talk to them about the impact and implications of their behavior. There is a lot of power in constructive interactions. However, we recognize that sometimes it is better to ignore the situation and walk away. It comes down to mental discipline and a lot of self-coaching. No one said it would be easy, but it is well worth the effort to acquire these capabilities.

> **As rational thinking humans, we can act independently; it doesn't have to be a locked in, cause and effect or automatic response.**

We read a fascinating commentary from Bob Schieffer, a CBS News correspondent and host of *Face the Nation*, about reality shows that thrive on individual competition and scheming. He said:

"What if there were a program that stressed teamwork instead of double dealing, a program where you somehow got points for putting the common good ahead of personal ambition?

I know it sounds crazy but I keep thinking that whatever gets done in this country, from little things like raising money to buying uniforms for the school baseball team, to big things like going to the moon, or winning World War II, gets done because people work together.

Americans have always admired those who inspired us to be more than we thought we could be, not those who schemed to take advantage of our weaknesses and sell us out. We mark George Washington's birthday, not Benedict Arnold's.

Isn't that a story that still has appeal? We could call it counter programming."

In an organization where competitive natures and personal heroics are the norm, imagine what could be accomplished if everyone channeled his or her energy, ambition, and passion into achieving immeasurable success for the team.

In Conclusion

The relay events in track and field have a remarkable team dynamic. Typically, each runner hands off the baton to the next runner in a designated zone. In some types of relays, this oc- curs as a "blind handoff." In this situation, the runner receiving the baton starts running down the track, reaches back with an open hand, and receives the baton from their teammate mid-stride. For blind handoffs to be successful, it requires practice, trust, and some type of communication plan so the receiver knows when to extend his/her hand. In most relay teams, runners are strategically assigned to their leg of the race or placement in the relay order, based on their unique strengths. Each team member adds value to the relay when positioned in a way that they can excel.

Now, compare this example to your own team. Does your team join together with good communication, trust, smooth handoffs, and the shared will to perform? What is good for the team will be good for you too in the long run. So find it in yourself to do what is best for the team, not just what seems to be best for you. Whether that is improving your contribution, being more flexible, or just enhancing your value, invest the time and energy to function at peak performance so your team can too.

CHAPTER

FOUR

Leader:
Teamwork Starts
With Great Leadership

4

Leader:
Teamwork Starts
With Great Leadership

Introduction

Elephants have great status in the Hindu culture and have been associated with royalty in India. If you study this large creature even for a short time, you will find many characteristics that, in a peculiar way, parallel characteristics of great leaders. Elephants are the largest mammal on land, and amazingly they have survived for 50 million years by adapting and adjusting to their environments across almost all of the continents. Elephants are extremely cooperative creatures. Despite their size, they rarely attack, preferring to steer clear of animals in their pathway, even small ones. Elephants can be very graceful; they have amazing balance, flexibility, and agility. Members of the herd will typically have close social relationships with and demonstrate compassion to each other. Remarkably, elephants are highly intelligent and have a significant learning capacity. It has even been found that they pass learning genetically through the generations. Some of the best team leaders we have seen and worked with are described the very same way.

Reflect for a moment on a leader you have worked with; or a leader from history you admire. What makes them great? What makes people willing to follow them? Great leaders are people who lead by example. They step forward when direction or help is needed. They are not afraid of hard work, and they immerse themselves in challenges to make the impossible happen. Leadership is central to a team's success so it is at the heart of the Diamond Model of Teamwork.

Machiavelli stated, "There is nothing more difficult to take in hand, more perilous to conduct or more uncertain in its success, than to take the lead in the introduction of a new order of things." Leaders run toward and attack, rather than avoiding problems, because they understand a sense of urgency and priorities. Team leaders share a vision with the people they lead. Leaders know that their own success, as well as that of the group, depends on the support and dedication of the people they surround themselves with. The Sullivan sisters (Denise, president of Campbell USA at Campbell Soup Company; Maggie, chairman and CEO of Citizens Communications Co; Colleen, Regional VP of Sales at Expedia Inc.'s Expedia Corporate Travel; and Andrea, Senior VP of Sales at AT&T Wireless) were encouraged at an early age by key leaders (parents, school teachers, etc.) to try, risk, fail, and above all LEARN. As you can see, leadership seems to flow in that family. We believe good teamwork is inspired by sound leadership qualities that include character, skills, and task knowledge. Team leadership means exercising positive influence that inspires individual members to willingly work together to achieve collective goals.

> **Leaders know that their own success, as well as that of the group, depends on the support and dedication of the people they surround themselves with.**

Shared Leadership

Some people on our own team believe that great teams begin with great leaders as opposed to outstanding members. However, the differentiating factor between effective and ineffective teams that we have worked with, hinges a lot on the person who assumes the responsibility for leadership. In the case of less effective teams, the appointed manager universally

Shared leadership requires willingness on the part of those on the team to step up and to take charge when the need arises.

emerges as the dominant personality and leader in the team. In effective teams, the responsibility for leadership is typically shared by many team members in conjunction with the formal leadership. Shared leadership requires willingness on the part of those on the team to step up and use their influence when the need arises. It also exists when the team is willing to allow members to have the opportunity to direct the team's activities in a particular situation. Exercising leadership is a conscious choice that a team member makes: whether to defer to the "appointed" leader or accept leadership responsibility and influence the actions of the team without waiting for a formal call.

So why is leadership shared in some teams and not in others? We believe there are three main forces at work:

1. The Organization

Exceedingly rigid or formal organizations tend to suppress individual creativity, judgment, and energy. Bureaucratic teams sacrifice these characteristics in exchange for conformity, predictability, discipline, and a false sense of loyalty and security. Certain elements undergird this narrow view of these organizations:

- Boring or uninspiring job descriptions
- Narrowly defined roles and responsibilities
- Strict rules and policies that are rarely challenged
- Rigid hierarchy or pecking order
- Lack of cross-training and too much individual specialization

When pushed to the extreme, these organizational principles drive out courageous leadership acts by individual team members who would otherwise see a need and try to fill it. The overriding thought is, "That's what the boss gets paid the big bucks for. Leadership is not in my job description."

2. The Person

"A true leader has the confidence to stand alone,
The courage to make tough decisions,
And the compassion to listen to the needs of others.
He/she does not set out to be a leader, but becomes one
By the quality of his actions and the integrity of his intent.
In the end, leaders are much like eagles. . .
They don't flock, you find them one at a time."

—Author Unknown

When things are not going well, it is too easy to place blame on the organization. Leadership is an act of courage. It takes stepping out, asserting yourself, and taking a risk. The ideal situation is to have team players who will assume a take-charge attitude when the need arises for their talents and insights. Shared leadership becomes essential when the team is facing a problem, a challenge, or adversity—not during periods of equilibrium or when the path ahead is smooth. Choosing to follow is safer than leading. Leaders empower others to act, but first they must feel empowered themselves; empowered to question and test their assumptions, values, self-confidence, need for security, and self-imposed limits. They are able to assert, to speak out, and to share their wisdom and inspiration. Leadership, like many elements of teamwork, starts with the confidence to overcome the natural internal forces that

> "Behold the turtle. He makes progress only when he sticks his neck out."
> – James Bryant Conant

keep individuals from taking risks, being courageous, being vulnerable, and assuming responsibility.

3. The Team

When the organization's culture, policies, and procedures foster individual initiative; or when individuals make a choice to assume leadership; potential forces within the team itself can short-circuit attempts to distribute leadership opportunities. Short-circuiting can also occur when other team members are unwilling to defer and let others lead, when only the loudest and most dominant voice takes the lead. When the standard operating procedures are such that one team member has to be number one and that promotions and recognition occur at the expense of other team members, justifying this uncooperative behavior is easy. "If I can't lead, then I refuse to follow" is a fair description of this phenomenon. It can also emerge when there is a low level of trust and respect between team members. Trust and respect are fragile and are earned over time through genuine actions. Without these qualities, attempts at influencing others will be frustrating and will foster a win-lose environment. Some other internal team forces that short-circuit shared leadership include:

FRAGILE

- Exclusive cliques

- Excessive pursuit of self-interests

- Unresolved conflict

- Blaming and finger pointing

- Jealousy

- Defensiveness

- Rumors, gossip, and griping

- Inflated egos and intimidation

Any combination of these forces will dissuade individual team members from assuming leadership responsibility. We see many work groups that are made up of higher performing individuals who haven't learned how to become a high-performance team. We refer to this phenomenon as the "curse of the brilliant." The curse is having highly intelligent individuals on your team, who are strong-willed, inflexible, and unable or unwilling to collaborate with anyone. If these smart people also have a dominant personality style, you end up with a group of brilliant people who can't problem solve together. The antidote for the team is to recognize these destructive behaviors and sit down face-to-face to openly resolve these concerns.

A common challenge that teams face when incorporating shared leadership into their team's practices is adjusting to the changing flow of leaders and role reversals. With each leader come different leadership styles, behaviors, traits, and skills. While distributing leadership responsibilities can cause temporary confusion and momentary setbacks, the benefits most often outweigh the costs. One benefit of team members taking the leadership role from time to time is an increased dedication and commitment to the team's

> **"Great achievement is usually born of great sacrifice, and is never the result of selfishness."**
>
> *– Napoleon Hill*

goals and overall success and a higher level of motivation to perform under other leaders when they have the role of team members. One of our colleagues, Cherissa Newton described being part of a project team in a service organization that operated very effectively under shared leadership. As new projects were assigned to the team, they met to collaboratively determine which team member was most capable of being the leader for each project. Because of the volume of projects the team was assigned, at any given time one individual could be both a leader as well as a team member. When asked about the team's success, she explained that shared leadership kept their team from getting into ruts and becoming too complacent with the way the team worked. Rotating leadership helped the team naturally challenge the status quo. This was especially beneficial given the creative nature of their work and their need to effectively problem solve with every project.

James Watson and Francis Crick were two fiercely competitive scientists. Watson, a zoologist, and Crick, a physicist, landed in the emerging field of molecular biology with hopes of uncovering the structure of DNA. Crick and Watson decided to work as a team to crack the code before anyone else. At the time, another team of scientists, Maurice Wilkins and Rosalind Franklin, was making progress towards uncovering the DNA structure using X-ray images of DNA. Unfortunately, the Wilkins and Franklin team fell apart due in part to some personality conflicts and tension, and Wilkins took the X-ray images to the Watson and Crick team without Franklin's permission. Once Watson saw the clear X-rays of DNA, he realized that the cross-shaped patterns meant the DNA was structured as a helix. Watson, Crick, and Wilkins ended up winning the Nobel Prize for medicine in 1962, laying the groundwork for the biotech industry. Relationship dynamics can be crucial to team synergy, or it can disrupt a team's mission, as it did with the Wilkins and Franklin team.

Encouraging Others to Lead

High-performing teams realize that leadership has to shift from one team member to another, depending on the task at hand. The appointed or formal leader knows that leadership can flow or transfer without a loss of prestige or power. Designated leaders or managers are really coaches, facilitators, and enablers who guide, advise, and help the team authoritarians. They believe their team members have tremendous untapped ideas and the potential to lead. They just need the right leadership style that allows them to blossom.

The style of the appointed leader should set the tone for leadership to emerge, so team members learn to influence the direction or approach the team will take. The following practices will foster the leadership skills of team members and encourage them to take the lead:

- Communicate the expectation of involvement and participation.

- Recognize and talk about others' strengths, knowledge, expertise, and experiences.

- Be less controlling and delegate often.

- Acknowledge and praise leadership contributions from team members.

- Be patient and let people have the room to experiment and learn.

- Be equally concerned with the team's effectiveness as with its efficiency.

- Invite participation by asking questions and drawing out knowledge.

- Ask people what kind of leadership helps them excel.

Leadership is not a position; you are not a leader just because you have the title. Leadership is something that is earned from followers on a day-to-day basis.

Leadership Close Up

Bill Bradley, All-Star basketball player and U.S. Senator, explained,

"Leadership means getting people to think,
believe, see, and do what they might have not

without you. It means possessing the vision to set the right goal and the decisiveness to pursue it single-mindedly. It means being aware of the fears and anxieties felt by those you lead even as you urge them to overcome those fears. Leadership can appear in a speech before hundreds of people, in a dialogue with one other person- or simply by example."

Whether you are a formal team leader or you are assuming leadership at a particular moment in time, our research has indicated that one's ability to lead is rooted in his or her effectiveness in nine key qualities. The first five qualities define who a great leader is; the remaining four define what great leaders do.

Humility

James Baldwin, an American writer, wrote, "The challenge of leadership is to be strong, but not rude; be kind, but not weak; be bold, but not bully; be thoughtful, but not lazy; be humble, but not timid; be proud, but not arrogant; have humor, but without folly." Great team leaders are humble and don't give in to feelings of superiority. A humble team leader defers credit for accomplishments to the team. Humility does not mean weakness. Great team leaders might be competitive and ambitious, but they channel those tendencies towards the success of the team rather than for personal gain. Ultimately, they recognize and appreciate what all team members have to offer today while remaining committed to helping them develop greater levels of contribution for the future. Displaying this quality is challenging in some cultures where great heroic acts and individualism are highly prized.

> **"Humility makes great men twice honorable."**
> – *Benjamin Franklin*

Conviction

Walter Lippman, a renowned journalist, wrote, "The final test of a leader is that he or she leaves in others the conviction and will to carry on." Tremendous personal will and determination to succeed are qualities of great team leaders. They work tirelessly, with great focus and persistence. Leaders with conviction can overcome challenges through consistent effort. They are willing to do almost anything to ensure the success of the team and expect similar commitment from other team members. We are not saying that to be a good leader you have to be a workaholic and give up balance in your life. What we are saying is that you need to be committed and focused day in and day out until the team achieves its

> **Leaders must be committed and focused day in and day out until the team achieves its desired success.**

desired goals. Leaders with conviction are passionate about their roles and responsibilities, their commitment to the direction, and their determination to help others succeed. Pat Riley, a professional basketball coach, put it this way, "To have long term success as a coach or in any position of leadership, you have to be obsessed in some way." We believe good leaders avoid becoming obsessed with power, status, and perks; they are able to control their egos.

A colleague of ours, Julie Ziadeh, shared an observation with us that she made while working with a leader who exhibited unrelenting conviction. While she was working for a major airline, a significant change in the direction of the organization occurred. For the first time in the airline's extensive history an outside leader, rather than one promoted from the rank and file, was brought in to manage the department of 20,000 flight attendants. There were critical and immediate challenges for this leader to address. Customer service ratings had been declining and a union was aggressively campaigning to organize this large flight attendant group. So the question for this new leader, Mary, was how to tackle the looming issues in a new industry and organization.

It seemed that from the first day, when Mary stepped into her new role, she had a strong sense of purpose. She built trust  and earned credibility with the flight attendants by deciding to go through five weeks of flight attendant training. She also knew that it was important for the flight attendants to get to know her. In fact, she refused to listen to the nay-sayers who said there was no way she could talk to all 20,000 flight attendants. But she did. She conducted 52 sessions over nine months across the United States. She used these sessions to communicate her vision, answer questions, set expectations, and promote open, honest, and often difficult dialogue. She then began to transform the organizational structure and work processes of this large department to ensure that her team had a line of site and accountability for serving the customer.

It seemed as if Mary had to continuously adjust her bearings, but her determination and direction never wavered. In 2001, the airline ranked number one again in customer satisfaction and in 2002 the flight attendants successfully defeated the union's attempt to organize.

Accountability

Arnold Glasow, an author, wrote, "A good leader takes a little more than his share of the blame and a little less than his share of the credit." Strong team leaders take personal responsibility for the good and bad results of the team and inspire accountability in others. Personal accountability means following through on commitments and rarely making promises that can't be kept. Accountable team leaders don't point fingers or place blame, but instead focus on what can be learned and how to make changes. By focusing on the "What" instead of the "Who," leaders make it possible for others to learn and improve without fear of blame. Great leaders create a spirit and culture where each team member accepts the responsibility to deliver needed results for the team.

Integrity

Medical missionary to Africa and Nobel Peace Prize winner Albert Schweitzer said, "Example is leadership." Credibility, honesty, and integrity are all descriptors of team leaders who are trusted; not just trusted in their abilities but also trusted in who they are. Credibility is built over time but can quickly crumble under breaches of trust. Leaders with integrity create a reputation of fairness and openness. Their relationships are created by example, exhibiting good judgment and common sense.

> **"Integrity can be neither lost nor concealed nor faked nor quenched nor artificially come by nor outlived, nor, I believe, in the long run denied."**
>
> *– Eudora Welty*

Peter Drucker said, "A man (or woman) might know too little, perform poorly, lack judgment and ability, and yet not do too much damage as a manager. But if that person lacks character and integrity—no matter how knowledgeable, how brilliant, how successful—he destroys. He destroys people, the most valuable resources of the enterprise. He destroys spirit. And he destroys performance. This is particularly true of the people at the head of an enterprise. For the spirit of an organization is created from the top. If an organization is great in spirit, it is because the spirit of its top people is great. If it decays, it does so because the top rots. As the proverb has it, 'Trees die from the top.' No one should ever become a strategist unless he or she is willing to have his or her character serve as the model for subordinates."

Courage

Rollo May, a psychologist, said, "The highest form of courage is the courage to create." Teams will not be successful if leaders don't give members permission to try new things, experiment, and at times fail. Risk-taking is an act of courage. Leaders have to be willing to stand up, speak up, and share what they think inside and outside of the team without being obsessed with the repercussions. Great leaders recognize the need to be a force in intentionally producing results, rather than just reading, analyzing, and second guessing the situations that arise. This means that a leader may be called on to make tough and even unpopular decisions. Courage is the will to act in spite of risks, dangers, or fear of failure for the purpose of team growth. Some people believe courage is an innate quality that you either have it or you don't. But, in actuality, courage is primarily learned. It is something that team leaders must seek out, study, and emulate in response to specific obstacles and defining moments. Great leaders generate courage in the moment and recognize when action is required, regardless of the risks involved. Courage can be refined, and it becomes easier through regular practice. Be dedicated to your vision, values, and goals while being willing to accept current reality and input from others. Courageous leaders are not afraid of making errors. Errors become mistakes when we fail to correct the error.

> **"Courage is not the absence of fear, but rather the judgment that something else is more important than fear."**
> – *Ambrose Redmoon*

Collaborate

Roger Simpson, Ph.D., Stanford University professor, wrote, "Resilience is really about collaboration and mutual understanding." Most team members have a need to be involved in and contributing to the success of the team. Great team leaders recognize and leverage this need by inviting, involving, listening, and being open to possibilities. This is illustrated by the Hindu fable, "The Blind Men and the Elephant," by John Godfrey Saxe:

It was six men of Indostan
    To learning much inclined,
Who went to see the Elephant
    (Though all of them were blind),
That each by observation
    Might satisfy his mind.

The *First* approached the Elephant
    And happening to fall
Against his broad and sturdy side,
    At once began to bawl:
"God bless me! But the Elephant
    Is very like a wall!"

The *Second*, feeling of the tusk,
    Cried, "Ho! What have we here
So very round and smooth and sharp?
    To me 'tis mighty clear
This wonder of an Elephant
    Is very like a spear!"

The *Third* approached the animal,
    And happening to take
The squirming trunk within his hands,
    Thus boldly up and spake:
"I see," quoth he, "the Elephant
    Is very like a snake!"

The *Fourth* reached out an eager hand,
    And felt about the knee.
"What most this wondrous beast is like
    Is mighty plain," quoth he;
"'Tis clear enough the Elephant
    Is very like a tree!"

The *Fifth,* who chanced to touch the ear,
        Said, "E'en the blindest man
Can tell what this resembles most;
        Deny the fact who can,
This marvel of an Elephant
        Is very like a fan!"

The *Sixth* no sooner had begun
        About the beast to grope,
Than, seizing on the swinging tail
        That fell within his scope,
"I see," quoth he, "the Elephant
        Is very like a rope!"

And so these men of Indostan
        Disputed loud and long,
Each in his own opinion
        Exceeding stiff and strong,
Though each was partly in the right
        And all were in the wrong!

As with the six men of Indostan, everyone, including leaders, has a partial picture of a given situation. Everyone is partly
right and partly wrong in their assessments, opinions, and
ideas. Collaboration requires a concerted effort to find the facts
and people who will contribute to a collaborative deliberation.

Team mates need to be willing to forego their own impulses
to solve problems and allow ideas and input from others to
surface. Collaborative leaders expertly combine differing opinions about "Elephant sized" problems that the team faces to
create a synergistic solution. Leaders should allow enough time
for research, discussion, and exploration to have a reasonable
expectation of finding the best possible solutions to team challenges and opportunities.

Align

Orway Tead, an author, said, "Leadership is the activity of influencing people to cooperate towards some goal which they come to find desirable and which motivates them over the long haul." Alignment may appear similar to "Direction" because it has to do with getting everyone on the team engaged in pursuing the team's defined mission. However, it is one thing to understand and be on board with the organization's mission and be completely committed to its goals (destination), but it is quite another to get people to agree on how to get there (means). It's easy for members to unwittingly be working at cross purposes even though they agree on the ultimate objective. Effective team leaders are able to clearly articulate expectations and opportunities for themselves and others and get them aligned on the best approach or methods to execute the tasks. Leaders who align their teams create an environment of cooperation.

> "To be a leader, you have to make people want to follow you, and nobody wants to follow someone who doesn't know where he is going."
>
> – *Joe Namath*

Enable

By enabling others, a great leader will develop a strong bench of effective team members and future leaders to call upon. You can get a sense of how well you are enabling others as a leader by asking yourself:

- Do your team members know what is expected of them every day?

- Do your team members feel as though they have all the resources, information, and authority necessary to fulfill those expectations?

- Do they feel accountable for their results?

Setting others up for success requires walking a fine line between giving freedom and flexibility while maintaining responsibility and order. Team members need clearly defined expectations, processes, and systems that allow the leader to monitor progress and ensure quality. Yet team members flourish when they have the freedom to find their own solutions to the team's challenges and are entrusted with a fair amount of autonomy and creative freedom.

Communicate

Author Karl Albrecht said, "The leadership challenge is to develop the idea, express it in compelling and useful terms so that everybody in the organization can relate it to his or her personal work life, and help them translate into action." Simply acting like a leader and going through the motions won't guarantee that team members will follow you. So one of the most important behaviors of great leaders is expertly communicating the causes they are advocating to the team members. When communicating, consider these points:

> One of the most important behaviors of a great leader is expertly communicating the cause they are advocating with the team members.

- Use appeals and ask other team members for ideas. Try an opening like, "I am not sure what the best way is to increase our commitment to the decisions we make as a team. But, I am willing to listen. Who has an idea?" This communicates a genuine willingness to explore alternatives and listen to others.

- Be empathetic and supportive. Team members have a stake in continuation of the status quo, especially if they helped create it. Recognize their feelings and accept their emotional reactions at face value, rather than denying the legitimacy of the feelings. Neutralize emotional attachment to the issues. Rather than denying that emotions have come into play, listen, empathize, and discuss them. A productive approach is to ask team members to consider how their emotional attachments may impact the discussion and progress with the endeavor.

> "The art of communication is the language of leadership."
>
> – *James Humes, professor, legislator, and author.*

- Communicate "conjecturally" or in "provisional terms," not in absolute black-or-white terms. "I am not sure what we need to do differently, but here is an idea to get our thinking going" is more effective than "No, you are all wrong about that; here is what we have to do." One statement invites conversation while the other creates polarization—a you-versus-them tone.

- Be descriptive and avoid accusations when discussing problems or setbacks. Statements or comments that are evaluative or judgmental tend to create a negative response in others. Describing what you see without a judgmental overtone is a more effective approach. For example, a pointed question such as, "Why can't we reach the results we need?" could cause other team members to defend their actions, rather than talk about the real obstacles. Use a descriptive statement to open the discussion: "We have talked about this situation during three meetings without any closure. How can we make the changes work and achieve the goals we set?"

Good leaders know the power of words; skillful communication helps team members see a leader as a positive force for improving the team. Team members feel more cohesive and can perform better when they are well informed about the goals, priorities, and progress the team is making, especially when the leader communicates this in an effective and artful way. Someone once told us, "Every time you speak you are auditioning for leadership."

The leadership style and actions of a historical figure can be instructive. This leader brought her organization from ruin to greatness. Following a tumultuous time of intolerance and prejudice under previous leaders, she became a leader admired by millions. She was explicitly clear about the reasoning behind her decisions and actions, so understanding and commitment to her leadership were enhanced.

These other notable practices and characteristics truly made her a great leader:

- She always offered her full support to others in both words and actions.
- She didn't seek vengeance against her critics.
- She learned from the successes and failures of her predecessors.
- She was able to integrate the comforts of the past with the needs of the time.
- She was confident in who she was and what she was charged with.
- She often counseled with advisers and sought the ideas of others.
- She regularly went out among the public to understand the realities of her people.

Her approach to leading her team has been described as, "[she] recognized that if you treat people you work with like robots . . . they will work like robots. Treat them as intelligent members of a team, and they will not only take an ownership pride in their work, they may well go about it more creatively."

This great leader was Queen Elizabeth I of England. Now we may not be leaders of nations, but we can aspire to be great leaders ourselves, position power or not.

We have found that while organizational cultures and styles may vary, the fundamental principles of solid team leadership are the same. High-performance team leaders perceive their work group as a team that is fueled by cooperation among its mem-
bers. They listen intently to team members, are sensitive to their needs, and actively encourage each member's participation. It all comes down to everyone on the team being willing and committed to share the leadership role, to rally the troops around a clear and compelling vision, and to stimulate high levels of team performance. Peter Drucker put it this way:

> **High-performance team leaders perceive their work group as a team that is fueled by cooperation among its members.**

> "Leadership is not a magnetic personality—that can just as well be a glib tongue. It is not about making friends and influencing people—that is flattery. Leadership is lift-ing a person's vision to higher sights, the raising of a person's performance to a higher standard, the building of personality beyond its normal limitations."

Conclusion

We have seen many extreme examples of poor team lead-ership over the years; you have probably seen them as well. But for the most part the majority of people really aren't bad leaders. Whether you are a formal leader or are working in a shared leadership situation, you likely have some untapped leadership abilities. We believe that with a little focus and ef-fort in enhancing personal leadership qualities and character-istics, whether a formal leader or not, we can all be better lead-ers. Perhaps not perfect, but we can make a significant differ-ence to our teams by being willing to be a great follower and a great leader. One team we worked with found the following leadership creed to be a helpful guide.

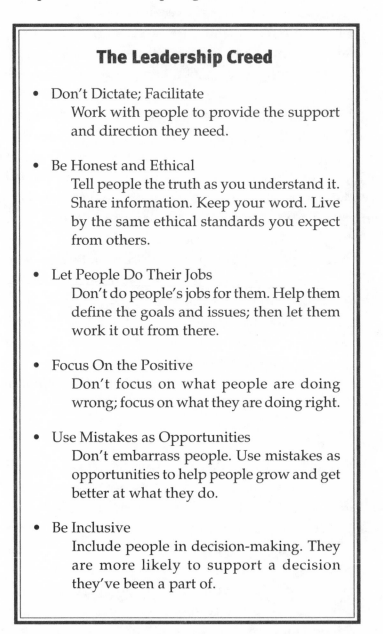

The Leadership Creed

- Don't Dictate; Facilitate
    Work with people to provide the support and direction they need.

- Be Honest and Ethical
    Tell people the truth as you understand it. Share information. Keep your word. Live by the same ethical standards you expect from others.

- Let People Do Their Jobs
    Don't do people's jobs for them. Help them define the goals and issues; then let them work it out from there.

- Focus On the Positive
    Don't focus on what people are doing wrong; focus on what they are doing right.

- Use Mistakes as Opportunities
    Don't embarrass people. Use mistakes as opportunities to help people grow and get better at what they do.

- Be Inclusive
    Include people in decision-making. They are more likely to support a decision they've been a part of.

FIVE

Direction:

Teamwork
Powered by Purpose

5

Direction:
Teamwork Powered
by Purpose

Introduction

Pine processionary caterpillars are perfectly named because they do exactly that. One caterpillar establishes a path and the others follow very closely behind and move in the same linear  direction. The leader makes all decisions about which direction to pursue and the followers' behaviors are so rote that their eyes become half-closed as they shut out the world around them.

An experiment by French naturalist Jean-Henri Fabre demonstrated the rigidity of the processionary caterpillars' behavior when he enticed the leader to start circling the edge of a large flowerpot. The other caterpillars followed suit, forming a tight, closed circle. The distinction between leader and follower became totally blurred, and the path around the flowerpot had no beginning and no ending. Instead of altering the nonproductive activity trap, the caterpillars continued their mindless path for several days and nights until they dropped off the edge of the flowerpot from exhaustion and starvation. Relying totally on instinct, past experience, and custom, the caterpillars achieved nothing because they mistook activity for achievement. As with the caterpillars, teams can get trapped in mindless activity and never really achieve what they set out to do.

In our Diamond Model of Teamwork, Direction is at the pinnacle of the diamond formation because a high-performing team breaks down the automatic "activity trap" and becomes specific about its vision, mission, and dreams. Everyone, not just the leader, has that target clearly in their sight. We have discovered through team interventions over the years, that successful work teams have one common element: all team members are working to achieve the same outcome. Building a potent team begins with identifying the core goal for all team members to focus their energy on. Having a well-defined goal helps answer the questions, "How do I fit, and why do I matter?" There is little difference whether it is a specific project, a department, or even the organization as a whole; each part needs to understand its purpose and role. The challenge in any organization is to get everyone's energies, talents, and abilities focused and aligned on a goal.

> **The challenge in any organization is to get everyone's energies, talents, and abilities focused and aligned on a goal.**

The former CEO of Porsche, Peter Schultz, illustrated this perspective in a story about having a compelling direction: "Three people were at work on a construction site. All were doing the same job, but when each was asked what his job was, the answers varied: 'Breaking rocks,' the first replied; 'Earning a living,' responded the second; 'Helping to build a cathedral,' said the third. Few of us can build cathedrals. But to the extent we can see the cathedral in whatever cause we are following, the job seems more worthwhile. Good strategies and a clear mission help us find those cathedrals in what otherwise could be dismal issues and empty causes."

A powerful team is like sailing on a long voyage. You need a good captain, crew, sturdy vessel, dependable engines, propellers, and fuel. But you also need some other components too: a steering wheel, rudder, and a precise destination. The ship would wander aimlessly without these components. Mechanically a ship could run efficiently, consume fuel, and keep the crew busy; but is it going somewhere of value? Direction is the steering wheel, rudder, and destination for a team.

In many ways, a team's direction should be a mirror image of an organization's mission and vision, but on a smaller scale. Unfortunately not all organizations have a clearly articulated vision, so a team has to grapple with its own definition of why they exist, what they stand for, and what they desire to become. So the question is, does your team know where it is going? If the question were posed to each individual team member, would there be consistency in the answers?

> **"There is nothing so useless as doing efficiently that which should not be done at all."**
>
> *– Peter F. Drucker*

Direction Defined

Like the combination of the steering wheel and cable connected to the rudder, plus a ship's course that has been carefully plotted, a team's direction has critical components too. Without all of its parts, the package is incomplete. For a highly effective work team, Direction consists of the following package of components:

1. **A Purpose:** The purpose defines what the team does (its business or function) and who it does it for. It describes the team's reason for being and exactly what its mission really is. It should guide, inspire, and motivate the team's work. A purpose is not strategy because it is something that is not "realized"; rather, it is a guide or aspiration.

2. **A Vision:** Vision is the defined future state for the team. It is the description of what success looks and feels like. It answers the questions, "Where are we going?" "What

dream are we pursuing?" and "Why are we doing what we are doing?"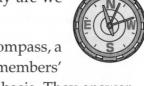

3. **Values:** Values serve as the team's compass, a set of principles that guides team members' behaviors and decisions on a daily basis. They answer the question, "What do we stand for and believe in?" Values identify the norms or guidelines about how the group is to work together.

4. **Strategies:** Strategies define how the team will mobilize itself to achieve its purpose and goals. Strategies detail specific results that the team will accomplish for long-term, sustained success. A strategy indicates the overall future position that a team wants to achieve and how it will get there. In other words, the strategy solidifies the "path" and the "place."

5. **Goals:** Goals are the measurable indicators of success. They are the jointly agreed upon mileposts to hit if the team is to make progress toward the final destination.

The combination of these five ingredients helps the team hone in on its Direction and becomes the mechanism by which teams achieve extraordinary results.

With a clear and compelling purpose, a team has a greater chance of becoming an unstoppable force. Despite an enormous bank of resources, expertise, and know-how, a team won't go anywhere without a shared direction that is stimulating and of course enduring. Imagine how much money, time, and effort are lost in organizations because a team's direction is confusing, vague, or not aligned with the larger organization's vision. Anemic teams, where the members do not have a compelling sense of purpose, rarely flourish. Yet, with some clarity a team can be something much greater. We once read an article about a pilot with a major airline who would fly long routes across the Pacific Ocean. He commented that an error of only 2 degrees in a 4,500 mile course (Chicago to Hawaii) would re-sult in the plane missing the destination by more than 145 miles. There would be no other landing sites until the plane reached Australia, which probably wouldn't happen since the plane would likely run out of fuel before it arrived there. Similarly, teams and the organizations they operate in cannot af-ford to have an unclear or misaligned di-rection, especially in a world that is shrinking and in which the global economy is increasingly competitive.

> "Our thoughts create our reality — where we put our focus is the direc-tion we tend to go."
>
> – *Peter McWilliams*

Benefits

In working with hundreds of teams over the past few de-cades, we have found that a clear and exhilarating sense of direction produces amazing results. As these teams publicly declare their collective intentions, they become much more fo-cused, aligned, and committed. Let us explain these benefits and examples further:

1. *Focus.* A clear direction provides a precise focal point to which team members can direct their energy. Members are able to recognize what the team's priorities are and can inquire about how they can contribute to it. People know what to do and why they do it. Their drive and tenacity are purposely focused.

2. *Alignment.* Explicit direction enables all team members to align their efforts, objectives, activities, roles, and re-sponsibilities and even attitudes, resulting in coordinated action. An aligned team member is invested in three ways:

    • Mind: Intelligence, skills, knowledge, techniques, un-derstanding.

- Body: Actions, behaviors, habits, practices.
- Heart: Personal values, commitments, beliefs, and assumptions.

A colleague, Bryan Yager, shared a personal experience he had with direction and the need for focus and alignment. One Saturday morning while doing some household chores, he was thinking about a teambuilding workshop he would be facilitating in the coming week. The team leader, his client, was frustrated with the squabbling that seemed to be taking place between several team members. It had been less than a month since the team's last off-site planning meeting about how to successfully complete a vital project. It had been a great meeting. They created vision and mission statements and identified what success would look like at the end of the project. They had clear goals and people seemed to be genuinely excited. It was obvious, the event worked wonders in pulling the team together. Now, just a short time later, things seemed to be falling apart.

While Bryan was thinking about what to do to help this team, his wife, Becky invited him to take a short break to go shopping with her. They decided that she would drop him off at a nearby office supply store and then go next door  to get her things. Just like the project team Bryan was helping, they had a vision, mission, and clear cut direction. They were in complete agreement about where they were going and what we were doing. They had the end in mind, so what could possibly go wrong?

His wife drove, winding her way through their neighborhood until she came to the stop sign at the entrance to their subdivision, she turned left and from Bryan's point of view, it was the wrong way. She was clearly not going via the most direct route. From his perspective, he promptly asked her where she was going. She responded that she was going to the office supply and craft store just like they had agreed. They began to debate which was the better route to take. Bryan was convinced his route was the most direct and therefore the quickest. She believed her route had less traffic and fewer traffic lights, therefore making her route the best idea. Despite the debate, there was a positive outcome. They both discovered that they each had valid points to consider.

After reflecting on that short shopping expedition, Bryan realized that he experienced something very similar to what his client was describing. It is actually a common experience for teams today. In both cases, there was clear agreement on the vision, mission, direction, and goals. Everyone knew where they were going, but each person knew a different way to get there. They assumed that having agreement on where they were going also meant they had agreement on the best way to get there. They were not aligned on the best way to achieve the shared goals.

Bryan couldn't wait to call his client the following Monday morning. It was a simple insight but one that he believed would help his client see the next steps for the team. The key learning point is that alignment is a must because a clear vision and/or goals may not be enough.

A team needs to work continuously for team alignment including how the goal will be achieved. This includes sorting through faulty assumptions. Having agreement in one area of a project does not mean that there is agreement in all areas. There is almost always more than one route to success, so teams must build in safe mechanisms and processes for people to share their personal methodologies or routes to success. You might be interested in knowing, that when there is traffic, Bryan turns left out of the subdivision when headed towards the office supply store.

3. *Empowerment.* Direction enables people to be empowered because they understand what the team is striving for. A group of empowered individuals can work in a self-directed manner, be innovative, and seize initiatives in many areas. They don't need to wait and be told what to do. Then, as milestones are reached, team members can make course corrections or receive recognition. As an added bonus, risk taking and creativity become normal occurrences. People gain confidence in challenging the status quo while knowing that everyone is working for the same ultimate purpose and operating with the same value system. We have discovered that as team members begin to feel empowered, they are more likely to make opportunities happen, rather than waiting for them to appear at their doorstep.

> **"An empowered organization is one in which individuals have the knowledge, skill, desire, and opportunity to personally succeed in a way that leads to collective organizational success."**
> – *Stephen Covey*

4. *Accountability.* Direction gives team members and team leaders something specific to be accountable for. A team's direction helps them take a greater interest in the work and fosters a desire to be more involved. Additionally, they are more willing to take responsibility without fear when results are short of the mark not just when things go right.

5. *Decision-Making.* Direction guides important team decisions, including the deployment of scarce resources. If more teams had extremely clear direction, teams would

be more proactive and spend less time reacting to problems or issues that arise. Improvements in processes, procedures, and systems would result from decisions made about how the work is organized. Direction provides a team with clear guidelines. We like to call it "chalking the field."

Too often leaders assume that a plaque or published document stating the team's direction will be enough. Or they assume that if they, the leaders, understand and believe it, then everyone else will too. But a team's direction must go beyond the team leader, and it has to be more than just a clever statement. The honeybee and its hive have a very clear mission: reproduce to populate the hive. In order to meet this mission, they have a fourfold plan: build a hive, protect the hive, sustain themselves with honey made from pollen and nectar, and reproduce. Each honeybee in a hive knows its role in this plan and fully dedicates itself to seeing it fulfilled.

One of our colleagues, Piper Abodeely, shared an example of a retail organization that discovered the benefits of and need for a clear cut and aligned direction. An executive team she was doing some consulting for had been stuck figuring out an operational issue for more than half of its weekly meeting. It was the type of meeting where no resolution was in sight. The team members were frustrated, defensive, and tired. Unfortunately, the weekly meetings had developed a regular routine: unproductive and ineffective.

In scanning the room, it was obvious to Piper that there was an apparent lack of team alignment, which in this case was inhibiting open dialogue.. The team members had become so focused on their individual needs that the critical mission of the team was overlooked and forgotten. Each team member had lost sight as to how they fit and why they mattered to the team and the entire organization.

Piper invited the team to look at their organization as a car and to identify which part they thought was symbolic of their role. For the first few moments there was silence, which quickly moved to chuckles and then progressed to laughter. What were they laughing at? Well, they had discovered how remarkably similar their roles re- **"Alone we can do so** sembled a particular part of a car. She heard **little; together we** everything from the wheels, gasoline, and **can do so much."** spark plugs to the engine and driver of the *– Helen Keller* car. People were not only naming their own parts of the car, but started to recognize how other people on the team filled certain functions of the car: "without the gasoline in the HR department, we would lack personnel," "If we were missing the control panel, we would have no streamlined operational measurements from the finance team."

As the team engaged in this spirited discussion, the members identified that they were missing part of the car: the steering wheel. What happens to a car without a steering wheel? What happens to a team and organization without a clear direction? This simple "ah-ha" addressed the lack of clarity and alignment within the team. Not only did the team begin to experience a paradigm shift, but the simple metaphor created the "space" for the team to re-examine themselves as a working system, and to recognize how each role is an integral component to creating a sustainable, high-performing team.

The exercise gave birth to a long-term initiative focused on answering the question "How can we guide and steer this organization so that it moves in the right direction and how can we make the changes we need, and do it in such a way that it creates high energy and yields extraordinary, sustainable results?"

Overtime, people saw the possibility of contributing to something larger than themselves. The emphasis shifted from focusing on why something can't be done to "How can we make this happen?" When the team began to understand how each individual contributes to the direction at a deeper level, members also recognized the value of interconnections among departments, processes, and people. As Rosabeth Kanter once observed, "Change is disturbing when it is done to us, exhilarating when it is done by us."

Getting Started

You may have seen the picture of two people laying railroad track from two different directions. The picture depicts what happened when they met without a clear direction. While the track is off by a minuscule distance, it is useless. Explicit and pinpointed direction helps the team effectively and, more importantly, accurately fulfill its purpose and put meaning in its values.

Unknown Source

While the concept of direction may seem straightforward, many teams unfortunately lack clear direction. When this occurs, chronic team problems arise and team members lose focus on meeting customer requirements and team-member needs. From our studies and work with teams, we have found that the number-one complaint from team members is, "We feel lost; we don't know where the organization is headed and what matters most." We often have these questions: "What should we do now? What is our next move? Who has a plan?" People asking these questions are clearly in need of direction.

So how does a team actually create direction? How does a

team define a charter or, as we like to refer to it, "a Coat of Arms", that defines the team's direction? The team Coat of Arms is the owner's manual to help the team navigate the future. Actually, direction typically is only one part of a comprehensive Coat of Arms. Though it can go by any number of names, some people call it an identity statement, a model, a code of conduct, an excellence agreement, a set of expectations, governing ideas, or ground rules. It really doesn't matter what it is called as long as a team has one.

> **"Synergism is the simultaneous actions of separate entities which together have greater total effect than the sum of their individual effects."**
>
> *– Buchholz and Roth*

It inspires and directs actions as well as recognizes positive behaviors from team members. The Coat of Arms helps to elevate the performance of the team. It speaks to important business and interpersonal relationship issues. This charter helps to create unity, alignment, and appropriate consistency because team members are able to invent and design the team of their choosing.

The team charter represents commitments and promises that team members share. Every team has a charter; it is just that some are spoken and documented, while others are implied and subconscious. Team Coat of Arms is rarely perfect. It needs continual renewal and updating to meet new situations, evolving roles, and expectations faced by each team. It will often need follow up and refinement; sometimes there are differences and conflicts but a Team Coat of Arms is worth struggling, exploring, and working out. We have outlined some ideas for developing a comprehensive Coat of Arms.

Create it

The process is fairly simple if you have a team that is functional and on solid ground. Gather the members of your team and discuss the following areas. Get their input and create some ownership. Have them work on it individually and then in subgroups. Finally, integrate the work of the subgroups into a consensus version of a Coat of Arms. If consensus can't be achieved on some point or if it needs some final wordsmithing, the formal leader can step up and make the call.

1. *Purpose*

   What is this team's singular reason for existence? For example, the unique purpose or role that binds this team together. It should be a shared purpose that reflects the products or services that this team supplies to the organization or its customers.

2. *Stakeholders*

   Who does the team serve? Who is it accountable to? What does its customers want and expect? Stakeholders are the people or groups who have major influence over the team's success.

3. *Vision*

   Where does the team want to be, and what will it be like when the team gets there? These can be broad terms, ideas, or aspirations stated in terms of relationships, results with customers and employees, and the environment or culture within the team.

4. *Levers*

   What are the key elements, levers, or variables that will facilitate the accomplishment of the team purpose and vision? What are the factors that will enable the team to be successful?

5. *Priorities*

   What are the four or five strategic priorities, actions, or chunks of work that will make a significant contribution to moving the team closer to achieving its purpose and vision? These are the specific things that "ground" the vision. Emphasize the distinct priorities that fit into areas that have not received enough attention in the past. They must be realizable, observable, or measurable in the next 12 or 18 months. These milestones must be deserving of complete commitment and the team's best effort.

6. Values

Values are deeply held views of what the team finds worthwhile and important. List at least three common or shared values which should guide the behaviors or actions of team members. These values show how team members intend to operate on a day-to-day basis with each other, customers, employees, and other stakeholders.

The following are some actual examples of team charters or Coat of Arms that articulate the direction of the teams.

Sample 1: Sales Team Charter

Vision	Be the #1 Sales Force in the industry • Committed to excellence, integrity, and improvement • Customer Focused
Mission	Secure a profitable business
Goals	Exceed our sales plans • Gross Margin $s • By individual, by region Improve sales productivity by 15%

Approach	Develop and execute sales strategies through regional offices
	
	• Focusing on the decision makers for operations budget
	  – Solving their key technical problems
	
	• Building a sustainable mix of business that includes
	  – Building relationships with new and existing customers
	
	• Consistently executing sales management disciplines
	
	• Support by world-class development & training

Sample 2: Manufacturing Team Charter

Our mission is to continuously exceed the expectations of our customers, employees, and community.

Our goal is to be the benchmark for excellence in every aspect of our business. We will strive to deliver perfect service through uncompromising commitment to continuous improvement.

Our promise is to create an environment of mutual trust and respect: to promote growth and personal freedom, to foster and renew teamwork and employee involvement, and to demand the highest ethical standard from ourselves and others.

We believe people are our most important resource and the foundation of our success.

To pursue our objective of "Serving Customers for Life," we are committed to being the acknowledged leader in our market for meeting the needs of our customers and employees.

Our commitment to this mission will make our team a place where people want to work and do business.

Invest enough time in this process so you can really begin to develop a sense of purpose and definition of what the future will look like. Once you have this foundation, you can begin molding your strategies, goals, and other performance measurements.

As you work through the fine-tuning process, use some passion, emotion, and energy. Make it global, optimistic, strong, and specific. A nicely worded direction is not enough; it must be compelling and excite people into action. It should inspire team members to perform beyond the traditional limits of their responsibility. The direction should stretch team members, yet give team members confidence and satisfaction in their work.

Commit to it

Once the direction is set, the next step is getting team members committed to and engaged in it. This is where the process can get daunting, as more than just an understanding of the common purpose and goals is required. Commitment is something much deeper. It comes from a sense of ownership and shared accountability. Jack Welch (CEO of General Electric) believed that the toughest job of a leader is communicating the vision and creating an atmosphere that inspires people to achieve it. Some commitment occurs naturally if team member involvement and input have gone into the defining the team's direction. If team members feel included, they will start to believe in the direction and invest themselves in it. Commitment is achieved one member at a time. It cannot be attained through a mandate or through force. When management or other members of the team over-control or dictate, the team member's commitment is squelched. We often see that when there is a lot of talk but not a lot of action; inevitably, a lack of zeal and individualistic behaviors and agendas return.

> **Commitment is achieved one member at a time. It cannot be attained through a mandate or through force.**

Live it

Once there is commitment and a sense of responsibility for the team's Coat of Arms, the collective energy of the team ignites. Team members begin to live it! It causes them to make sacrifices in order to achieve team goals, to make opportunities happen, rather than waiting for them to come along. They are more concerned about meeting the needs of customers and stakeholders. They have something concrete that they can be loyal to. So in your own teams encourage members to use it, refer to it, and reflect on it. Share information about the team's progress in accomplishing the charter or desired state. We have seen groups take a few minutes in their staff meeting periodically for team members to explain what the team's direction means to them. In the book Working, by Studs Terkel, results of interviews indicated that individuals in certain "extreme" professions or jobs such as nursing and education, work long, hard hours and yet remain positive and energized. Terkel believed that this happens because these individuals are convinced that their jobs have value and purpose: people are attached to a cause.

And Finally

Our own team spends time at the beginning of each year becoming clear and aligned about our priorities and goals for the upcoming twelve months. It is an important time for us.

> **"Vision without action is a dream. Action without vision is simply passing the time. Action with Vision is making a positive difference."**
>
> *– Joel Barker*

Once we have worked through the process, we distribute these priorities and focus areas to each team member. It serves as a visible and constant reminder of where we are going as a team. Our focus, decisions, and actions throughout the year are based on these key areas. To identify priorities and goals, we combine our knowledge from the past, assess the current challenges and needs, and anticipate future actions and efforts. Certainly we have to make adjustments and additions as our situation changes, but at any time our team members know what we are jointly working toward.

Direction is meant to elevate the performance of the team. Some aspects of it will need renewal and updates to meet the

changing situations and targets that the team will face, but it must be kept alive. Imagine a group of people in a deeply wooded forest wandering around in the darkness. A detailed vision of how the future should look and feel is like the sun lighting a path and serving as a compass that guides them through the deep woods to their desired destination.

CHAPTER
SIX

Community:
Better Together

6

Community:
Better Together

Introduction

Scientists have known for a long time that dolphins are extremely intelligent and social creatures. They typically live in pods, which have approximately 12 dolphins. They can also live in superpods, made up of multiple pods that temporarily join together, usually where the food source is abundant. These pods are flexible because dolphins commonly move to other pods. Pods of dolphins have been known to create strong, caring relationships with each other. They communicate using ultrasonic sounds, clicks, and whistles. It is remarkable how many parallels exist between dolphin pods and teams of human beings.

Webster defines community as a group or class of people having common interests, similarities, or identity living under some government. When we refer to Community in the context of the Diamond Model of Teamwork, we are talking about the relationships, culture, and environment that create a sense of kinship or special chemistry in a group of people that are working for a shared purpose. This description is similar to the way a pod of dolphins operates. The members of a business team we work with in the U.K. define community as, "A unified body of people with common economic interests, linked by common norms, policies, and locations." We believe team communities also have a spirit of fellowship, professionalism, and inclusion.

Think for a moment about the best team you have worked with or on. What was it like? How did it feel? Now, think about the worst team you have worked with or on. What was it like? How did it feel? Now if you contrast those two experiences, it is probably safe to assume that for most people the differences lie in the context of the relationships between members, the Community.

> **Community: A unified body of people with common economic interests, linked by common norms, policies, and locations.**

One of our colleagues, Magella Sergerie, shared a team community experience with us. In this real situation, numerous trainers and over 20,000 employees of a major bank were involved in an initiative to change the culture of the organization with regards to its approach to customer service. A team was formed that was comprised of senior trainers who would serve as mentors for many areas of the bank. This team of trainers became known for its excellent team communication as well as its approach to customer service. The team leader worked hard to keep team members informed about the needs and progress of the initative. Every member of the team diligently modeled good customer service techniques and skills at work and outside of work on a daily basis. It became a way of living for them. To be successful and ensure continuous improvement, they had to agree to coach each other on an ongoing basis. They tried not to take any feedback personally, but rather look at it as a development opportunity. In the spirit of good teamwork, they did everything they could jointly do to guide each other in developing and maintaining the level of customer service they were preaching in the classroom. Even ten years after that project, the team members still meet periodically to support each other and reflect on the good times all members of the team had during the important project.

Benefits

Everyone knows that blending multiple individuals with their distinctive talents, personalities, and perspectives into a  cohesive team is no small task. The Community part of the Diamond Model of Teamwork is an important piece of the teamwork puzzle because Community gives members a sense that they are involved in something greater than their own individual contribution. It enables the group to achieve more than if the task were left to individuals alone. In a true community, team members bring out the best in each other.

Community fulfills human social and affiliation needs because of mutually rewarding relationships. People innately need human contact, and when individuals are in a positive team situation, they naturally have this need fulfilled.

A close-knit community provides people with an opportunity to learn from their experiences, grow from mistakes, and heal from setbacks or problems. Team members are protective of each other so they can be empathetic and sensitive during challenging times or difficult situations. They trust and respond to each other with the utmost respect. When team members feel comfortable in their team situation, they are better able to fulfill their roles and responsibilities, persist through harsh realities, and confront personal challenges that arise.

A healthy community is a safe haven where team members can do their best work and be creative. In a healthy team, members adopt a covenant to be vulnerable, freely disclose information, and give constructive feedback to each other.

Some team members or leaders may feel that the culture of the team isn't important, that teams should only be focused on the task at hand. But, in actuality, when teams invest some time, thought, and effort in enhancing a supportive culture, the group will likely be more focused on the team's shared goals and be more productive. Too often, teams get distracted from the task because of unresolved community issues. Teams with a strong sense of community experience cohesiveness, cooperation, and coordination because they are capable of dealing with conflict and integrating the work of team members; they are also able to discuss the "undiscussable" as a group. Marvin Weisbord said, "Teamwork is the quintessential contradiction of a society grounded in individual achievement."

The Realities

We see a lot of teams with weak communities. The scenario is currently playing out with a leadership team we are working with on the West Coast. The team is dealing with two years of difficult markets, tough customers, and increased pressure from new competitors. Frustration is rampant, and bonuses have now been significantly reduced. Investors are asking questions about the anemic performance. People are pointing fingers, and everyone is jumping onto the blaming bandwagon. The solution is complex because there isn't one simple root cause. A lot of cooperation, trust, and communication will be required to unravel the problem and "right the ship." This is not the time for bad blood; in fact, this is the time when team community is needed the most, as adversity is raining down.

We are also working with other teams with the opposite problem. When the storms of adversity hit, they bond together, put differences and petty issues aside, and work collectively to get through the storm. But then when things settle down and they start growing and winning in the market, the daggers come out. They swipe at each other, and they seem to invent problems and complaints about other team members.

In many of our workshops we use a short questionnaire "What Workers Want." It asks participants to rank, in order of importance, a list of job characteristics such as compensation, job security, input on decisions, etc. Nearly without fail, characteristics related to relationships with co-workers and leaders are ranked within the top five. In fact, we recently learned

"No road is long with good company."
– Turkish Proverb

that when the questionnaire is administered in a retail context, relationships with co-workers ranked as high as second place. So it is really no surprise community issues like trust, communication, flexibility, and relationships are the source of more team problems than task related issues. The team may be composed of the most highly skilled and effective individual team members, but the team won't truly be high performaning if there are problematic relationships.

Community Close Up

The linkages between the elements of the Diamond Model of Teamwork are essential to successful team performance. This is especially true in looking at Community up close. For example,

 it is hard to imagine a close-knit team without solid team members who are competent and well-intentioned. It is equally hard to imagine a cohesive community without a leader who is willing to sponsor and support activities and processes that are designed to build and sustain team unity. Our research and practice in the field suggest that it is practically impossible to create a cohesive group of people who are willing to stick together through thick and thin without a common mission, a shared purpose, or a reason to belong. The team member has to have a clear direction and strategy to achieve a strong sense of community. It is hard to fathom team solidarity without mechanisms, training, and retreat opportunities to discuss important or tough issues and bring people together. As you can see, one element of the teamwork model, like community, can't be polished or repaired without paying attention to the other elements as well.

So what does a team need to do to take a group of talented individuals and create a cohesive unit? We believe there are eight things to focus on:

1. Team members need to have a clear responsibility and stewardship for the community that extends beyond their own individual job or field of expertise. Some people get very good at executing their individual responsibilities but can't or won't see how their efforts fit in the big picture and how they play a role in the development of the community. Team members have to devote some time and energy to the general welfare of the group, or they and the team will likely not reach peak performance.

   Building a team's community can be challenging for team members because teams consist of humans with different styles and with a range of affiliation needs. Building teamwork is not a one-time event; it must be a continuous, ongoing responsibility. The greatest danger for teams is when their members become complacent, having the illusion the community is in fine shape. They assume they are invulnerable to adversity and team-member challenges. This mode of thinking is like a ticking time bomb. An added challenge is sustaining community through ongoing organizational shuffles in direction and inevitable team-member changes and reorganizations.

   Over time, each team will have to discover, through experimentation, how to get team members to contribute in the creation of a positive community and then how to sustain it. The good news is that most community needs and challenges are solvable if every team member owns up to his or her contribution to problems, is vulnerable, and demonstrates accountability.

2. In great teams, members cultivate a desire to serve others and are genuinely concerned about others on the team. Everyone, at some time, will have a need; a time when he or she can use the help of others to succeed. When people over-book their time, have a rush of requests, or need help with a problem or a major decision, a strong community can really pay off. These are the moments when team members can and should turn to the group for collaboration and support.

The original Golden Rule says, "Do unto others as you would have them do unto you." The new Golden Rule says, "Do unto others as they would have you do unto them." That's right: as they would have you do unto them. This is a theme that has been used by many advanced cultures since ancient times. While it may sound odd, it should be central to every team. Many problems and conflicts arise in teams because team members have selfish interests or focus on their own goals and needs rather than the needs of others or the members collectively. Support and concern for team members' well-being are like a safety net for a trapeze artist. They give other team members the confidence to do what they need to do and persist through challenges. Think about how much more comforting it is for a team member to take risks, be creative, and become interdependent if they know other team members are looking out for them and cheering them on.

Do unto others as they would have you do unto them.

We read once of a small company where this principle was central to the operation. When a long-time employee of the organization, a woman who cleaned the office weekly, was diagnosed with cancer, the team wanted to support her. They decided to clean the office themselves so this team member could continue receiving a paycheck until she was healthy enough to return to work.

3. In order to create community, team members have to break down destructive cliques and subgroups. As team members, we have to be conscious and aware that we may gravitate into special-interest subgroups. We have seen certain inner circles where members always go to lunch together and never include others; and other members who always sit together and take the same position on key issues during meetings. It is nearly impossible to create a community if these little alliances exist and refuse to let others in.

Many of Aesop's fables apply to teams. The fable, Father and Sons is a poignant example:

A Man had several Sons who were always quarreling with one another, and, try as he might, he could not get them to live together in harmony. So he determined to convince them of their folly by the following means. Bidding them fetch a bundle of sticks, he invited each in turn to break it across his knee.

"In union there is strength."

– Aesop

All tried and all failed: and then he undid the bundle and handed them the sticks one by one, which they had no difficulty at all in breaking.

"There, my boys," said he, "united you will be more of a match for your enemies but if you quarrel and separate, your weakness will put you at the mercy of those who attack you."

So what does it mean? There is strength in union, and union comes from team members working together cohesively.

4. Another way to build a team's community is to create opportunities in meetings, lunches, off sites, and training sessions for people to have a bit of fun and get to know others at a deeper level. Sometimes we call it serious fun. In other words, real work is being done, but the exercises, tasks, and activities require people to mix together, share information, or connect with other players on the team. One of our colleagues, Dr. Richard Williams, shared a real example of how this works. He believes that once a person has been a team member on a real team that person will be spoiled forever. Although there are many reasons why a person can feel "spoiled" by serving on a real team, one of the strongest reasons is that real teams create a profound sense of belonging, harmony, team identity, team cohesion, and a sense of community.

> **"Fun is only real and sustainable if it feeds off the team's purpose and performance aspirations."**
> *– Katzenbach and Smith*

His example of being spoiled happened in a road construction company near Cleveland, Ohio, in the mid-1990s. A cross-functional group of employees had been asked to serve on a process improvement team for the purpose of revamping the paperwork that moved throughout the organization. Six team members represented sales people and estimators who bid on and secured projects, engineers who ensured technical compliance and accuracy, construction supervisors who managed the projects, office staff who provided support, and the field people who did the actual construction.

For over a decade there had been a feud in this organization between the field and the office. The field crews didn't believe the office staff had a clue about what they were doing and clearly didn't understand how to build roads. And the office personnel didn't understand why the field people were so strong-willed, opinionated, uncooperative, arrogant, and uncompromising.

From the first few minutes of the first meeting, the cross-functional team struggled to even discuss simple issues such as when and where to hold their weekly meetings. The memory of past feelings between office versus field interfered with the communication process to the extent that basic decision-making and interpersonal trust seemed impossible. At one point, when the team appeared to be stalled, the CEO of the company attended a meeting and literally pleaded with the six team members to "forget their differences and work together."

The CEO's plea had a limited effect on the team members. They continued to argue and disagree over the simplest of decisions, and at one point the decision was almost made to abandon the process improvement project altogether. But the company's need to improve communication and paperwork flow between field and office was so pressing that team members were asked to continue meeting and strive for improvement.

At times, personal differences among team members can be bridged with some really simple gestures like sharing a treat or snack. Diana, the office manager and team leader, began taking various treats to the meetings. She started with chips and her personal salsa, but soon graduated to more interesting selections. One such treat, Swedish meatballs, was a huge success. The team began talking about what foods they liked and disliked. Then Diana began one of the weekly team meetings by saying, "Before we get started today, let's go around the room and tell each other something we do outside of work for fun."

Each person shared a hobby or activity that was considered fun. A civil engineer found out, for example, that he and a construction superintendent both had a passion for hunting; in fact, they both hunted the same area during the same hunt each year. Diana learned that a construction foreman had a passion for BBQ. Diana and her husband had recently become Certified Barbeque Judges. Their similar interests in BBQ started a discussion that ended with them sharing favorite recipes and restaurants. Gradually the discussion turned to the assigned task of improving the paperwork flow with a little more openness and respect for each person's position.

At the beginning of the meeting the following week, Diana asked each team member to share an embarrassing experience. She related a time a few years earlier when she dumped a box of popcorn in a person's lap in a movie theater. Several of the other team members followed suit by relating similar mishaps. After sharing several laughs together, the team again moved to the paperwork-flow issues, this time with even more willingness and openness to dig deeper into the issues and consider new possibilities.

Over the next few weeks, Diana put different team members in charge of the snacks. The CEO allotted the team a small sum of money for each team meeting for treats. Snacks became an important part of each meeting, as team members tried to outdo each other in finding the most appealing snack. As the weeks progressed, the team members began to talk and agree more, while disagreeing and complaining less. Members of the team found common ground not in the business process they had been asked to improve but in the personal things they liked to do. They connected on a personal level first, and then they were able to communicate respectfully on a professional level.

What the team developed were feelings of community. Effectively communicating on a personal level opened up for the team members, the possibility of communicating professionally at a deeper level. When team members communicate effectively, they begin to understand each other; understanding others enables appreciation of others. Appreciating different positions leads to respecting opinions of others, and respecting others opens the door to interpersonal trust. When interpersonal trust abounds in a team, the members share a feeling of community, which can lead to the achievement of uncommon results.

> **When team members communicate effectively, they begin to understand each other; understanding others enables appreciation of others.**

When the team members Richard worked with in Cleveland overcame their personal differences and developed a sense of community, they successfully overhauled the process in which information flowed from office to field and from field to office. The solutions created by the team members were shared throughout the organization, and the following year the company enjoyed its best performance of its 40-year history. After the team's work had been concluded, Diana said she would forever be spoiled by the experience because the feelings she had from team community were so profound that they would stay with her forever.

5. A cohesive team will share the responsibility for creating linking and bonding opportunities. One organization we have worked with for many years on the East Coast is a good example. The team is predominantly male, and the young and very talented female members felt excluded. As they put it, "the good-old-boy-network" has been through the wars together and is tough to break into. For the men, it was a real blind spot, and they were sometimes in denial about the fact that the community hadn't jelled. The leader of this business division followed our counsel and started having members of the team who were not in the inner circle plan their semiannual team retreat. As a result, the senior male team members gained an appreciation for the work and creativity of the newer and younger female members. In turn, the talented women no longer had an issue about exclusion because they became the focal point and decision makers for the agenda and activities for the offsite community building meetings.

Regrettably, in many organizations, teams have lost a lot of human contact and bonds. The influx of technology, e-mail, and virtual offices doesn't do much to build a team's sense of inclusion. Team members need to adjust and focus on productive opportunities for interaction with each other. Technology should be used as a resource for achieving cohesion, rather than a barrier to opportunities to make critical team connections. A team can make

Team members need to adjust and focus on productive opportunities for interaction with each other.

progress just by recognizing and understanding that face-to-face communication and linkages are imperative to the team's future success.

During the American Revolutionary War, people as far away from each other as Massachusetts and South Carolina had to speak in one voice if the colonists were ever going to break away from England and defeat the most powerful army in the world. The New England colonies, Middle colonies, and Southern colonies all had different ideas of what the new country should be fighting for, but they were able to bridge their individual interests and recognize how important it was to join together, accept individual differences, and build unity for a common purpose.

6. Team member actions and behaviors that exceed expectations need to be recognized, celebrated, and reinforced.

    We know of a team where one team member experienced a painful surgery with a long recovery period. She was unable to travel long distances. One of her colleagues assumed her role on some crucial projects. This involved some personal sacrifice and inconvenience for the team member filling in, but it made the entire organization look flawless in the eyes of the customer. It was important for their team to recognize and celebrate the great contribution of the team member who stepped up for the good of the whole team.

    > **"A group becomes a team when all members are sure enough of themselves and their contribution to praise the skill of others."**
    >
    > *– Anonymous*

When establishing a reward, base it on team productivity as well as individual performance. Group-wide rewards will add to the strength of the team's community.

7. Trust should be the cornerstone of all team-member relationships. Trust ensures productive, satisfying, and long-term relationships. Team members should communicate with constructive candor and avoid gossiping and its repercussions. They should actively listen to each other and support decisions and agreements. Basically, they need to "walk the talk."

> **"Trust men and they will be true to you; treat them greatly, and they will show themselves great."**
> – *Ralph Waldo Emerson*

We have observed that trust can be difficult for teams to develop, yet it is easy to lose very quickly. Even when established over an extended period of time, it remains dependent on predictability and consistent behavior. Bottom-line, trust paves the way for strong relationships and team cohesion.

8. A team needs to be able to candidly talk things over, coach each other, and share important feedback. A community-oriented team raises essential issues, openly discusses them, and then finds collaborative solutions. But rarely do teams talk openly about their reactions and feelings to each other. Most people withhold feelings, even in close relationships, because they fear hurting the other person, making him or her angry, or being rejected. Because most people don't know how to openly share constructive feedback with others, they don't say anything at all. Then the other person continues on, totally unaware of the effect his or her actions are producing in others. As a result, many team-member relationships that could be productive and enjoyable gradually flounder

and sink under the accumulated load of annoyances, hurt feelings, and misunderstandings that were never openly discussed.

Community Obstacles

As is true with any of the elements in the Diamond Model of Teamwork, obstacles can stand in the way or complicate a team's community. When these situations arise, leaders and members need to develop solutions quickly so negativity or issues don't spin out of control and drive people away. Here are some common red flags to be on the lookout for:

- People who glorify in task accomplishment at the expense of others

- Team members with extreme or aggressive personality styles

- Team members who are excessively shy or feel awkward

- Team members looking to fill their ego needs

- Interpersonal inflexibility

- Self-interest and greed

- Team members who draw attention to themselves

- Team members who feel superior to others

- Impatience and a need for immediate results

- People who simply refuse to try to get along with others

- Compensation structures that reward competitiveness between team members

These are some of the most common root issues that lead teams to their demise. It is often little things that go unaddressed and quickly fester into serious problems.

It can even be a difficult task for sports managers to get their players to focus on what is in the best interest of the team rather than their own statistics. Dealing with large ego needs and players who don't believe in what the manager is trying to do often stifles any growth from a struggling team into a team that has community. The World Champion Anaheim Angels were able to build team community during the 2002 season and ended up winning the World Series for the first time in their 42-year franchise history. The manager wanted to instill in the players a sense of willingness to give themselves up for the greater good of the team. Instead of always trying to hit home runs to score, he asked the players to just try to get on base and let others on the team hit them in for runs. In the mindset of baseball players, nothing looks better on the stat sheet than a lot of home runs, so the Angels' team members didn't "buy in" to this community approach right away. They got off to their worst start in franchise history and forced the manager to call an emergency team meeting. After that, everyone began to realize what the overall result would be if team members would join together. When individual members of the Angels look at their stats from 2002, they might not have the most home runs they have ever hit, but they do have a World Championship.

A Final Thought

High-performance teams work at building spirit and commitment; they talk about how they are doing, and they are willing to invest time, money, and energy to protect and enhance the basic team fabric. In a productive team, people care about each other and are concerned about how their actions and attitudes affect each other. We like to think of a team community as a close-knit neighborhood.

> **"The nice thing about teamwork is that you always have others on your side."**
> – *Margaret Carty*

Good neighbors protect and look out for each other. When a child wanders off, everyone joins in a search. People notice if strangers are in the area and they pay attention when lights are on at odd hours. People loan and return tools to each other; people pitch in and help clear snow from sidewalks and driveways. The community knows what kind of help others need. People are simply comfortable and familiar with each other. It seems that these picture-perfect neighborhoods are be-  ing lost to a world in which everything is fast-paced and in which people are more secluded and isolated. But teams and organizations can't let this happen. Good teams have good relationships; they know how to build them, and they know how to maintain them. We need more organizations to step up and commit to the team approach—TEAM: **T**ogether **E**veryone **A**chieves **M**ore.

SEVEN

Structure:
Teamwork By Design

7

Structure:
Teamwork By Design

Introduction

You may remember the racehorse Barbaro, known for winning the 2006 Kentucky Derby. He was a heavy favorite to win the 2006 Preakness Stakes, but only a short distance into the  race he fractured three bones in and around the ankle of his right hind leg. Despite valiant efforts by vets, owners, and even the horse himself, he eventually could not be saved. But in spite of his tragic end, there is an interesting connection between what occurred biologically to Barbaro and a team's structure.

Barbaro and other racehorses are bred to optimize the horse's speed, rather than durability. So when Barbaro lost the ability to stand on his right hind leg as a result of the injury and six subsequent surgeries, he naturally shifted his entire body weight from four legs to three. Some healing did take place in the injured leg, but complications developed in the front legs, a condition called laminitis, as a result of bearing the weight of the horse's body. This ultimately led to Barbaro's sad, untimely demise.

A team must also have a balanced structure, where team members have clear roles and responsibilities and distribute responsibilities in an optimal way for the team's success. If the structure is fundamentally broken or if some members are not fulfilling their parts, the team can absorb the weight for a time, but ultimately the entire structure has to be balanced, or the team, unable to bear the weight, will find itself with unfortunate complications that will lead to its downfall.

From the beginning of time, tribal, religious, and military organizations have all figured out ways to determine who does what in order to hunt down food, cross a desert, defend the high ground, or build a magnificent cathedral, synagogue, or mosque. Teams of people will always be needed to engage in spectacular endeavors like conquering space, curing horrific diseases, or mastering the information age. So for teams to succeed, they need to figure out how to divide and organize the work. In modern organizations, it is common to find a wide variety of teams: functional and cross functional teams, task forces, customer teams, sales teams, R&D teams, process teams, and many more. While some teams accomplish their work within an existing hierarchy, others are loose and often informal federations of people. Depending on the size of the team and the nature of the work, the team may be structured with a clear leader and team members or it can be a more self-directed and autonomous. Keep in mind that all teams are at different stages of development and different levels of effectiveness, which can complicate how teams divide up the work.

In some form or another, everyone is involved with a team. If you are a manager, you most likely have a team that you lead. You may be part of a team with other managers, and you may even be in another cross-functional team or task force. Beyond that, you may also be part of a family, faith, sports, or community-service team. We could go on, but in life we typically serve on multiple teams that are driven by needs for performance, service, accuracy, speed, and responsiveness. Because teams are so prevalent and we are involved in so many teams at various points in life, it is crucial that teams have a solid framework that will enable its members to be clear about what and how they can contribute to their teams' process and purpose. Structure is also critical from a personal perspective because our job or role defines who we are. Many people identify with their job—it means everything to them.

When we refer to structure, we are primarily talking about roles, responsibilities, duties, and assignments that team members fulfill. In addition, structure defines the broader function of the team as a unit within the larger organization. Structure also refers to the controls, measures, and accountability that must accompany the roles and duties. A team's structure is essentially made up of two factors: primarily the "It" or the work of the team, and the "I," or what each individual is responsible for as part of a collective effort.

Teams build a solid structure by defining all of the roles and responsibilities team members must fulfill and how these roles will be integrated. Structure includes allocating the work to individual team members and defining how they will interdependently and independently contribute to the team's purpose or function. Not only do team members need to know what duties, responsibilities, and tasks will be required of them, but they also need to understand how they play a part in the big picture and how they can personally add value.

> "The strength of the team is each individual member... the strength of each member is the team."
>
> – *Phil Jackson*

You may be familiar with one of the original U.S. comedy duos, William Abbot and Lou Costello, who are most recognized for their hysterical routine entitled, "Who's on First." Their performance centers on the game of baseball, and the act features an exchange between a peanut vendor and a fictional baseball team manager. The vendor (Costello) asks the manager (Abbott) "who" is playing on the team. But this is where the confusion about the baseball team's structure begins. The manager replies, "Who's on first, What's on second, I don't know is on third." Confused, the vendor replies, "That's what I want to find out." The lengthy dialogue continues about who is filling the baseball team's roles because what the vendor doesn't realize is that the player literally named "Who" is on first, the player named "What" is on second, and the player named "I Don't Know" is on third. While this is quite a humorous, fictional situation, many real teams have a lot of confusion about who is covering the team's bases, and it is no laughing matter, especially if there is a tight deadline, a furious customer, or a lean budget to manage. Clear, defined, and understood structure is the solution to this challenge.

Benefits

Highly effective teams have clearly articulated roles and responsibilities. This produces efficiency, coordinates effort, and reduces confusion. Good structure also eliminates the unnecessary duplication of work that can be so detrimental, costly, and inefficient. When individuals are clear about the contribution they need to make and the contribution the team as a whole needs to make, the following results tend to occur:

- The team members realize greater fulfillment and job satisfaction.

- There is less duplication of work.

- The team members contribute more value to the team mission.

- There is greater retention of talent.

- Matching and selecting new members are much easier.

- Members work more efficiently and are more dedicated to the team.

> **Highly effective teams have clearly articulated roles and responsibilities.**

- Members focus on integrating their work with the work of other team members.

Authors Brian Mennecke and John Bradley researched structure in teams and reported their findings in their article entitled "Making Project Groups Work." Their research found that teams with assigned roles and responsibilities resulted in increased group cohesion, higher quality of work, and more positive experiences.

Structure Close Up

Imagine a crowded buffet with hungry people. It can be pandemonium as people bump into each other, walk in every direction, and occasionally cut in line to reach the dessert bar. Structure helps teams create order without reducing all the fun and spontaneity. Now imagine a group of team members who are crystal clear about what they are expected to do and accept it. This will probably lead to a better result for everyone involved.

As a team explores the roles and responsibilities of its members, it has two overriding aims: (1) clarity, and (2) coverage. Clarity means that each member understands his/her personal duties, responsibilities, and behavioral expectations required to complete individual tasks. Coverage means that tasks, requirements, and results that the team is expected to produce are being addressed once all the individual contributions and roles come together. Team members are collectively responsible for the tasks to be covered, so gaps in roles and responsibilities can be detrimental to the team and its ultimate success.

> "You don't get harmony when everybody sings the same note."
> – Doug Floyd

Whether you are forming your team's structure from scratch, reorganizing a team, or if you just want to tune up the roles and responsibilities of your current team, there are a few fundamental steps to follow. In an existing team, this is a good exercise to ensure proper coverage and distribution of the team's work and the greatest contribution of every team member. Sometimes periodic change in the team's structure is necessary for teams to fulfill their mission. It is important for the right people to be in the right places doing the right things. Whenever possible, team members should be involved in formulating the structure of the team. We find that team members are more committed to fulfilling team expectations and are engaged in the work if they are included in creating or refining the team's structure. There are seven essential steps in developing sound team structures:

1. Define Roles and Responsibilities

The first step is for a team or its leader to define the exact roles and subsequent responsibilities, duties, and job tasks required of each team member. This is really defining "what" each team member does. It has long been understood that for people to be engaged in and passionate about their work, their roles and responsibilities need to have sufficient meaning, variety, importance, and freedom. These factors should be included when defining each team member's roles and responsibilities.

It is totally appropriate to allow team members a degree of flexibility within their roles and within some reasonable guidelines. Avoid situations where individuality and creativity are squashed in an attempt to have perfect order, achieve every efficiency, and reduce every redundancy. Defining the non-negotiable choices and actions, as well as the areas where individual choice and flexibility can occur, is critical. Role flexibility allows creativity and innovation to emerge, as well as opportunities for team members to develop skills beyond

> "I long to accomplish a great and noble task, but it is my chief duty to accomplish small tasks as if they were great and noble."
>
> – *Helen Keller*

their current responsibilities. This helps enrich the work and provide intrinsic job satisfaction. A team should consider the appropriate challenge and complexity of each role and match them to the capability of each member. Try to create a structure where people do a "whole" job, not just repetitive and uninspiring pieces of a larger task. The key question to ask is, "Do the roles and responsibilities tie directly to the accomplishment of the team's collective goals?"

2. Define Knowledge and Skills

In addition to defining roles and responsibilities, the team or its leader must dig to a deeper level and clearly define the competency requirements for each member and each job. These are the knowledge and skills required to fulfill the responsibility (what the team member has to do and what he or she needs to do). These skills and competencies should stretch beyond the typical technical skills found in a job description and include competencies such as technical problem solving, interpersonal skills, or organizational know-how.

3. Provide Authority and Tools

Next, consider the tools individual team members need to effectively fulfill their responsibilities and unleash their motivation. We are referring to levels of authority, resources, tools, technology, training, or development opportunities that are central to effective execution of the duties and tasks. Without having the capacity to obtain the critical tools and resources needed, team members won't be able to execute their assignments or maximize their potential. What's more, they will become frustrated in knowing that they could achieve more if they were better equipped.

The proper amount of authority emboldens people to stretch, create, and be entrepreneurial about their work. This concept is often referred to as the authority scale:

Authority Scale

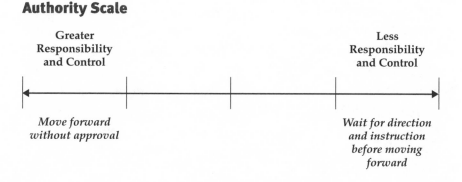

On one end of the scale, team members have a great amount of authority as it relates to their specific roles and responsibilities. The other end represents situations where team members have limited authority over their responsibility areas.

4. Match Team Members

Once teams have defined the ideal structure (roles and responsibility areas), the time has come to match team members to the team's clearly defined goals and mission. Optimally, the team should assign roles to team members in a way that capitalizes on versatility and opportunities for cross-training so everyone is capable of performing a variety of tasks and can back each other up in emergencies. This reinforces the team's community. Each team member's role should be matched to the individual so he or she can add value and assist in the ongoing improvement of the team itself. Fundamentally, the assigned roles should leverage the skills, natural abilities, and expertise of team members.

At this point in the development of the structure, assumptions should be avoided about the limitations of any one team member's experience or ability. The focus should be on gaining a complete understanding of everyone's strengths, weaknesses, and ability to step up and work a level up from their routine jobs and responsibilities. As an added bonus, understanding team-member capabilities will produce valuable information on development needs and knowledge gaps to be filled. Team leaders should use the matching process as a basis for coaching members and planning for future growth and advancement opportunities. Matching team members and tasks effectively will result in a collection of team players who blend together well, create extraordinary results, and experience personal fulfillment from working together.

5. Communicate and Get a Commitment

After matching individual team members with what the team needs to accomplish, it is extremely helpful to communicate to the team how the structure is designed. Most importantly, this dialogue helps build people's commitment to fulfilling their roles and responsibilities like a well-oiled machine. The crucial link here is communication. Team members need to fully understand the purpose and importance of their roles in order to make a full commitment to the team's mission.

> **Team members need to fully understand the purpose and importance of their role in order to make a full commitment to the team's mission.**

Commitment will be stronger if people know the answer to "How do I fit and why do I matter?" People also want to know how they can apply their knowledge and capabilities to do their jobs and contribute to the team's goals. We have found that team-member commitment increases when members "own" their roles rather than just feel assigned to them. Ownership requires not only knowing what to do, but also understanding the level of authority and responsibility that go with that role.

By anticipating, communicating, and providing all of the critical information about role expectations, you are supporting people's successes and unleashing motivation. You need to be confident that all team members know exactly what is expected of them and how their work integrates with the work of others. Not only do they need to recognize which responsibilities are unique to them, but also which ones contribute to the overall functionality of the team. Too often we get busy or distracted and fail to set people up for success by clarifying what is uniquely their responsibility and what they are empowered to do.

6. Set Personal Goals

This is an appropriate time to build in mutually agreed upon performance targets related to individual team roles. This process is most effective when individual goals are aligned with organizational strategies and priorities. Again, the key with performance targets is to solidify goals and objectives. This means using the SMART (Specific, Measurable, Attainable, Relevant, Time-bound) framework to ensure that everyone fully understand their personal goals and plan of action.

7. Coach and Maintain Accountability

Finally, the structure of a team won't be sustainable long term without ongoing support, coaching, accountability, and review. In any team, team members will experience setbacks or challenges within their areas of responsibility, requiring coaching and feedback from peers, leaders, and stakeholders to help them reach their full potential. This is a check-and-balance process that will protect the team and team members from ambiguity and chaos.

Ongoing adjustments and renegotiation of duties and performance targets are required to achieve optimal performance. Flexibility and willingness to adapt, as well as awareness of areas where ongoing coaching and development can occur, will open up opportunities for added responsibility or advancement in the future. And, of course, personal accountability is the tie that binds this all together. Without some methods or mechanisms, team members will have nothing to answer to if they are not fulfilling their commitments. Accountability will be discussed in more detail later in this chapter.

Using these steps to obtain clarity and thoroughly cover the team's requirements can take some effort and time as the structure is created, renewed, and revitalized. However, it will be time well spent and value added long term for the team and the organization. It is vital to get this structure element right, so explore various alternatives, and make multiple attempts if needed to determine the best structure for your team. Remember, be proactive and don't be afraid to experiment or flexibly respond to changing needs. But it doesn't stop here. A team needs to consistently explore the structure from a strategic perspective by asking, "How will our structure need to be different to strategically fulfill the team's responsibilities and customers' needs in the future?"

Structure Obstacles

Team leaders and team members must ensure that team responsibilities are divided effectively and fairly, even though situations may arise where people work outside of their defined boundaries. For example, we once received a large order for materials that was needed by a customer in a short time frame. We used this as an opportunity to gather our entire team, and as a group we all worked closely together to fill the customer's request and meet the deadline. It was a great cross-functional learning opportunity for our team members, and it increased our team unity as we quickly completed an urgent project. Our team members understand that there are times where everyone has to pitch in and help someone if the team is to be successful. Having the flexibility to take

> "In the end, the only people who fail are those who do not try."
>
> – Anonymous

on additional responsibilities outside of their primary roles is built into their mental framework and they are committed to performance excellence in all of their responsibility areas.

We can't emphasize it enough: disputes and role contention will surely arise if team members don't understand what they are fundamentally responsible for at a personal level. When these situations occur, conflict can build on itself, causing strife, reduced productivity, and increased dissatisfaction. Role clarity is particularly important during the forming stage of a new team.

In a team we work with, there are two individuals whose responsibilities overlap to some extent. To further complicate the situation, when one or the other is extra busy, the other individual is expected to step in and assist. We found that while it builds the spirit of teamwork as they work together to get a job done, in actuality, things sometimes drop between the cracks and furthermore, other team members are often unclear about where jobs stand or who to go to for information. Not only are the two team members impacted by this situation; everyone on the team must also know the role boundaries and how responsibilities overlap. Then there needs to be an ongoing process of communication about changes or adjustments in roles and responsibilities.

Another challenge facing teams is helping the members take full ownership for and commit to every responsibility they have been given, no matter what it is. Team members can't just do what they are good at or what they enjoy. All responsibilities need to be filled, even the unpopular, uncomfortable, or disliked tasks. These responsibilities can only be ignored for so long before they create a lot of ambiguity and eventually, if left unaddressed or unassigned, will

Everyone needs to do his or her share of the difficult and unpleasant duties that are inevitably a part of every team.

start to take a toll on the team's results. Everyone needs to do his or her share of the difficult and unpleasant duties that are inevitably a part of every team.

Role conflict can also occur if team members don't fully understand how their responsibilities fit into and affect the "whole." As we mentioned earlier, it may require clearly defining how the work of the team members is integrated into the "big picture" if they are unable to visualize it on their own. Oftentimes, people will be excellent "silo" workers in fulfilling their own independent roles but lack the vision and accountability to integrate their piece of the work with the work of others which is the key to maximizing operational effectiveness.

In our own organization we call this phenomenon "comprehensive thinking." As individual team members fulfill their assignments, duties, and tasks, we challenge them to considerer how their actions and work may be impacting other aspects of the team that may not be apparent on the surface. We want our team members to think beyond the basic focus area they have and explore how their assignments, as little or big as they are, fit into the larger mission. These considerations make a differ-ence in our long-term success. Sometimes this doesn't happen, and when people drop the ball it is because they are only focused on their immediate task, they don't understand that thinking beyond the immediate task is also their responsibility, or they just get busy.

Finally, you will need to monitor and coach those members who are too possessive of their turf and won't ask for help when they need it. They may simply be insecure and unwilling to share tasks, insider knowledge, and problems they are encountering.

Accountability

Think for a moment about a time when you realized you were a key part of a problem or situation. Did you realize on your own or did someone tell you? How did it feel when you learned about it? What did you respond to?

Accountability is all team members taking full responsibility and ownership of their roles and their performance. It means acting in a respon-

Accountable team members align their actions with personal, team, and organizational values.

sible way, despite the outcomes or consequences. In a solid team structure, team members are accountable to the team as a whole as they fulfill their duties and responsibilities to the best of their abilities. Accountable team members are open about their contribution in good times and bad. They align their actions with personal, team, and organizational values.

Team members are held accountable through performance expectations. Without a means to monitor or track successful or unsuccessful performance, there is nothing concrete to hold team members accountable to. Now reflect back to the questions earlier. Were there specific expectations in place in your situation that helped signal when things were off track or to help you know something needs to be changed? Clear standards and expectations help team members monitor their own performance and accountability and make things easier for team leaders or team members when performance feedback or change is necessary.

Whatever approach you utilize (coaching opportunities, mentoring, performance appraisals, performance reviews, etc.) to help maintain accountability, be sure it monitors individual performance and allows for specific coaching and feedback on a regular basis. The last thing you want is team members going down the wrong road and then discovering they are off track. Remember, the entire team's success is only as strong as the combined performance of each team member. At the very least, each member deserves to know what he/she will be measured on and accountable for their performance.

Accountability has to be consistent. One person can't be held accountable for something while the same thing slides by with someone else. That will inevitably cause problems with the team. The best approach is to make accountability equitable for everyone.

Just to reiterate, the key here is matching individuals to tasks and to capitalize on their individuality, but not at the expense of cooperation! Getting the right people in the right seats on the bus can make or break the team's ability to accomplish its mission.

Conclusion

Structure is much like the framing of a house. Each element of the framing, (timbers, braces, and trusses) fulfills a critical role. Some framing divides a house into individual rooms, while other framing serves as bearing walls that support the roof. The same applies to a team: people contribute to and support the achievement of the operation through the individual roles that they play. If the structure of a house is well designed and built with good craftsmanship, it will fill its intended purpose and withstand the elements over time. A well-designed team will do likewise.

Structure is one of those real "nuts and bolts" elements of the Diamond Model of Teamwork. Much of it is not visible and lies hidden below the surface. However, if the framework of roles and responsibilities is wrong, a team will never achieve the precision and quality needed to serve customers and deliver quality services. Just like in the construction process, the frame sits on the foundation, and the rest of the teamwork elements are linked to the frame; it is all tied together.

EIGHT

Process:
Getting the "It" Done

8

Process:
Getting the "It" Done

Introduction

One of the authors grew up in the country and had a fascination with all kinds of living creatures, including ants. As a boy he ordered an ant farm from a mail order house. It was fascinating to watch them learn how to operate and adapt to the environment during cold snowy days. Ants are powerful little creatures. Left unchecked, a colony of ants can cut a fairly large swath through a forest. Ants seem to subscribe to some rules, processes, and guidelines that apparently are hard-wired to their biology and allow them to create engineering marvels.

> "Ants are good citizens, they place group interests first."
>
> – Clarence Day

Generally, ants live in large colonies and have an internal structure of roles that enable them to share their food and their work. Some ants act as housekeepers, picking up trash and depositing it in a trash room; some act like the police and maintain order. Other ants are nursemaids that watch over the nursery room in the colony, and others are tunnel miners, gardeners, and herders. We find that watching the work that goes on in an anthill is the most interesting dynamic in the insect world.

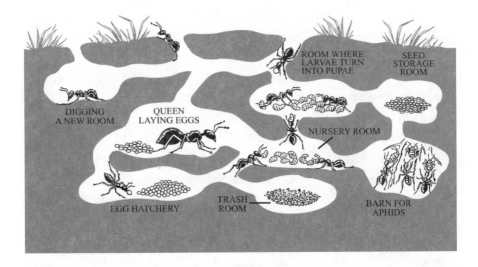

In many ways, ant colonies are similar to human organizations: they work, play, and keep pets. Although small, they are incredibly strong. Often, ants will team up, two or more, to drag a caterpillar that is several times their weight back to the colony. Female ants do all the work. The males do nothing except mate with the queens (unfortunately, after mating, they die). The workers (females) clean, gather food, nurture the young, and defend the colony against external threats: lizards, toads, spiders, birds, and weather. Without question, the queen is the leader in the ant hierarchy. She starts the organization and calls the shots. Ants are so effective in their work that some scientists believe that without natural predators, there would be far too many ants to deal with on earth.

If an ant stumbles upon a good food source (grubs, sugar, honeydew, a crumb, etc.), it grabs all it can carry and heads back to the colony or nest. Often the ant will stop a colleague passing by; the two have an ability to communicate with their feelers. The fortunate ant, the one that has discovered the food source, seems to say hurry up and leverage the opportunity. The teammate then picks up its pace and joins in.

Other ants are like supervisors: they urge the workers on to carry as much food as possible back to the colony in their "extra stomachs." These are sometimes called the "social" stomachs because ants are willing to feed others in the colony from their team stomachs. It makes the point that even lower life forms create organizations and teams with roles, structures, and processes for their leaders and members.

The word process means different things to different people. Webster defines "process" as something that is going on (progress or advancement of some kind). Webster also indicates that a process can be an "organic or natural series of changes leading to a result; in an organization it means actions or operations directed toward a particular outcome."

Process: Organic or natural series of changes leading to a result.

In the context of the Diamond Model of Teamwork, process is a protocol, mechanism, or operation that enables the team to function at peak performance. A team's processes are helpful and agreed-upon activities, procedures, or methods that have been incorporated into the team's way of conducting business. They represent a unique way of accomplishing its work or mission. The processes govern how a team goes about doing the "It" (team task requirements) referred to earlier in the book.

Processes are like the intellectual property of a team. If all the teams in an organization are brought together, along with their processes, the result is the makings of an organization's unique, competitive advantage.

Benefits

Teams with well-defined processes reap many benefits. Processes pave the way for consistent and predictable results, which are critical for teams that operate in fast-moving and chaotic environments. These teams may have a strategy that is in flux or have extremely high-quality demands. Solid team processes offer big payoffs when a team is facing critical obstacles or serious setbacks. Their processes pave the way for clarity, direction, and results because they don't have to be debated; the teams accept the process as the best practice until they learn otherwise. High-performing teams don't make it up as they go; they think through the actions and activities that will create efficiency and results.

Clearly articulated processes give team members confidence and guidelines to operate in, which, in turn, emboldens members and produces a sense of empowerment, ownership, and responsibility for the work being performed. Processes encourage synergy, participation, sharing of innovative ideas, and creative problem solving. Good processes monitor and track the work being accomplished and help provide feedback for the team on its progress and necessary adjustments. Processes contribute to the long-term, sustained success of teams.

Process Close Up

Try to imagine a modern world without processes. Picture a medical system, hospital, or operating room without processes. Imagine getting to work each day without some procedures or "rules of the road." Try to picture a pilot landing a plane at a busy airport without clear-cut protocols, procedures, and accepted rules. Try to imagine going into a coal mine without having standards and consistent safety methods. As organizations become more complex, the planet gets more crowded, and our actions intersect with the actions of others, the need for clear-cut processes becomes critical. Two hundred years ago it might not have been as important: people had a lot of space and flexibility to pioneer across wide spaces and to improvise on their own. But even then, if you wanted to cross the ocean in a tall ship, there were some procedures that the crew had to agree on and support in order to cross a treacherous body of water safely. Today, virtually every endeavor, every profession, and every work group need work guidelines as well as rules that govern both the behavior and the steps needed to complete work in a relatively consistent manner. Without them, we are left with a rather chaotic situation or even anarchy. Obviously, the organization would achieve no worthwhile results.

> "The world of reality has its limits, the world of imagination is boundless."
>
> *– Jean J. Rouseau*

Processes, however, do not preclude problems. Processes can cease to be helpful when they become bureaucratic, cumbersome, redundant, or irrelevant. As teams change, processes must evolve and adjust. As new technology emerges, teams need to incorporate it and continuously improve. When processes hinder the group's effectiveness, it is a signal that a process needs to be changed, discarded, or a new one invented. Value-added processes require a balancing act between convention and invention, between change and tradition. The team has to collectively determine when it is time to abandon or modify an accepted process, or design new ingenuous ones.

It is all about coordination and collaboration. A process represents the proverbial "box" that is talked about a lot in business. We implore people constantly to think and act outside the box. In the case of teams, we want people to **"think"** outside the box first, before they recklessly **"act"** without using a defined process of getting agreement from the group about how to proceed. Clearly there is a time to experiment, explore the boundaries and norms, and contribute new process ideas, but the team needs to agree and be synchronized before a process or a "new box" is installed.

The challenge for teams is honoring and respecting status-quo processes while reinventing, changing, testing, and innovating with new processes. Once again, imagine the outcome if someone in the accounting department independently decided to change accepted accounting practices and "cook the books?" What would happen if someone chooses, on his or her own, to circumvent the legal code or alter safety procedures for a medical device or drugs? There can be costly, even life-threatening outcomes when innovation and ingenuity are not synchronized with tradition and convention.

Two Major Types of Processes

Helpful processes that regulate and govern team activities fall into two fundamental categories. The first category comprises the mechanisms or processes that are essentially task or technical in nature. They facilitate the execution of the work itself by focusing on how the work can be performed effectively and efficiently. Processes in this category are largely non-human things such as work-flow protocols, procedures, and policies. They also include the rules and regulations that have been adopted to achieve safety standards, quality, consistency, speed, continuous improvement, planning, budgeting, and measurement of results. These processes help people keep track whether the team's tasks are being accomplished or not.

They include these elements:

1. Mechanisms for the productive and efficient flow of work

2. Protocols to meet safety standards

3. Processes to measure results

4. Administrative procedures

The second category focuses on the human element. These processes are designed to help people interact, coordinate, and integrate their efforts. They include these elements:

1. How information will be shared

2. How problems will be solved

3. How decisions will be made

4. How conflicts will be resolved

5. How grievances will be addressed

Specific examples of both task- and human-oriented processes include the following:

TASK-ORIENTED PROCESSES	HUMAN-ORIENTED PROCESSES
Operational Protocols	Team ground rules
Project reviews	Meeting ground rules
Work reviews	Performance reviews
Innovating techniques	Team retreats or development initiatives
Work logs	Team value systems
Process maps	Standards for customer interactions
Kaizan events	Mechanisms for information sharing
Reporting requirements	Conflict resolution steps
Accountability measurements	Reward and recognition systems
Quality standards	

Helpful processes can even take the form of rituals and customs that the team has adopted to support people in doing the things that require joint effort. We will share specific examples of a task—as well as a human-oriented process at the end of the chapter. As you can see, processes can vary and cover a wide variety of areas. Yet, they all have one thing in common: they improve the functionality and the tactical effectiveness of a team.

Another way to understand processes is from the perspective of complexity vs. simplicity. Processes can be simple, relaxed, and informal, or they can be complex, precise, and very formal. They can be documented, recorded, and prescribed, or they can be informal and even unspoken customs that have been discovered and accepted. Some processes are virtually innate and subliminal in nature, like those of the ants we described at the beginning of the chapter.

You may remember the very sad and tragic event that occurred when the USS Greenville collided with a small Japanese boat full of young students learning how to fish. This unfortunate and unnecessary event killed nine people off the coast of Hawaii in February 2001. The mistakes which led to the tragedy resulted from a failure to rigorously follow the submarine's processes and procedures. About 20 minutes prior to the collision, an important procedure was cut short. This procedure enabled sonar to accurately locate surrounding ships. Because the vessel was behind schedule, the leader and team members were less thorough with their processes than normal. When the commander ordered the ship to periscope depth for a final scan a short time later, he did an "80-second 360 degree sweep" rather than conducting his usual three-minute scan. He cut the process short even after noting earlier in the day and again at the time that there was a "white haze" over the water. The commander announced to his team that there were no visual contacts and they could begin to surface. The lack of accurate information from the sonar combined with the abbreviated surface scan led to deadly results when the submarine collided with the 60-yard trawler, Ehime Maru.

While processes for your team may not be as critical or lead to such devastating outcome, the message still applies about how important it is to have well-defined processes that everyone is committed to and will execute completely, even when time is at a premium. People have to speak up when processes are not being followed. Sound judgment is often reliable, but it is better to have time-honored processes and human judgment working together.

> "Companies should decide what processes and competencies they must excel at and specify measures for each."
>
> – *David P. Norton & Robert S. Kaplan*

Teams with good processes function like well-oiled machines. These teams don't have too many processes that bog them down in bureaucracy and mediocrity; neither do they have too few, which could lead to confusion. High-performing teams spell out their processes and document them clearly; step by step, so they are easy to understand and follow. People get trained on the team's processes, and the processes are reviewed and maintained over time so they remain relevant and value-added. Even well-oiled machines need to be tuned and overhauled from time to time. The Blue Angels flying team is renowned for their finely tuned processes. They have both a world-class team and technical process that allows them to fly precise formations. We most enjoy their signature formation known as the "Diamond" with its precise measures. The Blue Angels team reviews, studies, critiques, and hones these processes until they are a real art form. The Blue Angels provide many clues about how to do processes the right way.

Process In-Depth

So how do you improve or create a good process? First, you have to observe the current operation and measure the results your team is producing now. Even if you aren't aware of them or haven't documented them, your team has processes. In other words, if you are achieving something you are going  through a process. If you are achieving your mission and you are on track with the direction you have set, then your internal processes are likely in pretty good shape. If your stakeholders (customers, management, and other teams in the environment) are satisfied with your performance, you are probably on the right path. If not, it may be a red flag that processes are out of sync with the realities and needs of the business.

Secondly, you need to engage the team; bring them together since they are closest to the work and let them problem solve and diagnose the disconnects or inefficiencies in the processes. Again this is an area where the Blue Angels excel. They check and review the process before and after every show.

Third, set a clear value-added objective or outcome for each process. If there is not a clear value-added outcome, there is really no need for a process. Processes have to serve a purpose or need. The following list represents the needs a process might serve:

A. Effectiveness (ensuring achievement, the desired end result)

B. Efficiency (facilitating optimal utilization of resources-time, money, equipment)

C. Quality (consistently producing services and products that meet or exceed requirement specifications)

D. Safety (protecting the health of people and the environment—workers and consumers)

E. Motivation (enriching the work experience for team members)

F. Coordination (promoting information flow and collaboration)

Fourth, in order to be functional or useful, processes have to be mapped out and defined by the team. If you can't define the process, you can't manage it.

Fifth, people on the team have to commit and buy into the process; people have to own the process and own the responsibility for improving or changing it when necessary.

Sixth, you have to measure compliance, individually and collectively. People need to get feedback and coaching on their efforts to support and use the processes according to the agreements in the team. In essence, members need to conform to process standards.

Seventh, processes need to be reviewed, modified, and improved on periodically.

We have been working with an R & D team that has been poorly led for over five years; its processes are in desperate need of streamlining and improvement. All the stakeholders, including customers and other team members, suffer from an-

> **"The great thing in this world is not so much where we stand, as in what direction we are moving."**
>
> – *Oliver Wendell Holmes*

tiquated and outmoded procedures. Their intellect and expertise haven't been used effectively. People want to be efficient and they are anxious to have an opportunity to overhaul their processes using a team approach. In the short period of time we have worked with this team they have begun to make significant progress. In fact, they have been meeting regularly in what they call "Blue Angels" meetings to work out process

bottlenecks and inefficiencies. It is exciting to see their dedication to process improvement with this approach.

Keep in mind that processes will vary greatly depending on the type of work the team does and where the team is positioned in the organizational hierarchy. Teams in the heart of the organization, close to the core work, will have a blend of processes. Some will be task and technical in nature, and some will be focused on human interaction and human dynamics. As you move up in the organization, the focus of the team shifts somewhat from task execution to task planning, strategic management, and the organization's culture. For example, the processes of a senior leadership team would be focused on relationships, team dynamics, strategy formulation and renewal, etc.

Cautions

Although, some processes in many teams may be implicit, a high-performance team needs processes that can be articulated by team members because they cannot effectively implement what they don't know or can't describe very well. The last thing a team wants is to have team members in a position where they have to guess what the process is. This can unfortunately lead to inconsistency or costly mistakes if they guess wrong. Of course, sometimes things naturally work out when people improvise, but a team will be better equipped for success if team members don't have to make assumptions about the best way to execute a task.

What happens in most teams is that over a long period of time their processes emerge naturally and become clear, but this can occur at the expense of efficiency: team members are spending valuable time, and possibly wasting resources, trying to figure out what the rules, boundaries, or procedures are, rather than having explicit pre-defined processes and systems in place. Gradually, team members will learn where the lines of demarcation are, but teams benefit from investing some time to articulate the processes they will adhere to.

As a team works towards establishing and clarifying critical processes, it is helpful if the following points are addressed:

- What the process is for

- How the process impacts team members (how it fits into their roles and responsibilities)

- What the benefits are for using the process (for the individual team member and for the team as a whole)

- What the consequences are for using or not using the team's processes (obvious or unknown, positive and negative)

One team we work with gradually neglected a key process and suffered a lot of pain because of it. This team provides a critical service to a lot of other teams in the organization. However, they did not stipulate or communicate to their internal customers how to submit requests to get some technical work done. Consequently, the team's clients flooded them with requests, all of them were priority one of course. It proved to be very frustrating, even demoralizing not to have a process in place to approve and prioritize the work requests. Once this was resolved, the team's performance and morale improved dramatically. Many leaders busy themselves recreating, redesigning, or reviewing their processes, but unfortunately the team members, who in essence are the key people in executing the processes, are actually left out of the review or creation. When this occurs, they may not understand the rationale behind the process and will likely spend more time questioning it than implementing it. As you have probably seen or experienced, team members tend to get impatient with or reject what they haven't been involved in creating or what they don't own themselves. Teams get more mileage from processes by involving as many people as possible. With accurate clarification and involvement the team will achieve proper execution. Team members then feel that their views have been heard and that they own the process. Although time consuming, commitment to the process is enhanced because the team members were part of constructing it.

> Teams would get more mileage from processes by involving as many people as possible.

Maintain and Sustain

Just because a team has a process doesn't mean it is helpful or will make it easier for the team in reaching its goals. Processes are creations of people, so they need to be scrutinized and creatively modified so they always support the functioning of the team and the efforts of team members. When not kept in check, the wrong processes can cause more problems than they were intended to solve or, even worse, aggravate other processes that may normally be productive. When evaluating the viability of current processes, the team should ask these questions:

- How did our current processes become what they are today?

- What processes continue to serve our team well?

- What processes could be reduced or streamlined?

- What processes could be expanded or applied in other areas?

- What processes could we create?

- What processes could we eliminate?

- What processes will we need in the future?

The beauty of reducing or eliminating processes is the team begins to move away from crippling bureaucracy and towards a nimble, self-empowered, and self-directed work team.

To answer these important questions, teams can scrutinize recurring problems, customer criticism, bottlenecks, and time-consuming areas of responsibility. Teams can also investigate the helpful processes that other teams, divisions, or departments utilize. Delving a layer deeper in how the team operates and examining specifically which processes are helpful to the team and which are less helpful can be an eye-opening experience that will greatly enhance your teams success.

We worked with an organization that had a process for project management. While it looked good on paper and made sense on the surface, they found it was actually becoming a hindrance in practice. In fact, it took a new employee speaking up and saying, "This is too redundant, complicated, and frustrating" before anything was done about it. Later, through careful evaluation and discussion with the entire team, they were able to zero in on the duplication and gaps that could be modified and then pinpoint exact areas that needed changes. Now, the process is working well, and ironically this mechanism is being used more frequently, to the team's delight. Improving processes is the responsibility of every team member. The team culture needs to be such that team members are comfortable speaking up and challenging the way the team operates.

Conclusion

Of course, good team processes take discipline and commitment, but in most cases they correlate strongly with how well a team performs. The challenge is not to just get team members to commit to utilizing the processes, but rather for them to champion the processes. Champion is defined as "Someone who defends, supports, and promotes a cause." It has also been said, "A championship team is a team of champions" who know how to work together.

Bottom line, the solution can be simple. When it comes to processes, keep them simple, make them known and make them better. Henry Ford said, "Coming together is a beginning. Keeping together is progress. Working together is success." Process is all about the tools to help teams work better together.

Task-Oriented Process Example: Policies and Procedures

Policies and procedures processes can be a necessary evil because when designed properly, they strengthen the team; on the other hand, they can jeopardize the success of the team when they are mismatched with the team's needs.

There is no magic solution to finding the right balance with policies and procedures. What we have found is that it takes collaboration among team members to create effective, simple, and streamlined guidelines and principles for ensuring a well-oiled organization. We emphasize simplicity, but not at the expense of clarity or rigor. Teams must consider including policies and procedures that are mandates of customers and the nature of the operating environment.

Mission-critical policies and procedures need to define the operating boundaries and address the important rules that will guide the team to success while avoiding dangers, traps, or problems. Again, they should serve the team's mission, not hinder it. With appropriate boundaries to guide the team, confusion, chaos, and unwanted surprises will be avoided.

Human-Oriented Process Example: Team Ground Rules

One of the most critical human-oriented processes that a team should undertake is defining and subscribing to ground rules or behaviors that will enable the team to stay on course. This process serves as an insurance policy and hedge against future problems. Ground rules tie all of the processes together. We are referring specifically to operating ground rules, not just meeting ground rules, although there is some overlap. Ground rules not only establish a strong base for decision making but also for the way the team functions—a code of conduct for team members, if you will. We find that most teams have ground rules, but they have never fully defined and crystallized them. In fact, this can be an easy and productive thing to do and will ensure long term team alignment. Ground rules can address all types of topics, but they primarily fall into four key areas.

The first area is ground rules that enable team members to have a safe haven to participate in. Specifically, these types of ground rules address appropriate language, respect for others, and valuing diverse viewpoints and backgrounds. They may also speak to team members' willingness to be open and vulnerable, support each other, persist in open dialogue, and listen until solutions are found and problems are solved.

The second area to consider when establishing team ground rules is team-member contribution. Each team member should understand and feel personally responsible for contributing to the success of the team. Ground rules help the team member do this through timelines, follow through, reliability, and being fully present and participatory in group discussions.

The third area is ground rules for making decisions and gaining consensus. These address things like the brainstorming process that will ensure all ideas surface and are heard. Teams must ensure that discussions don't turn into "blame" storming. Ground rules in this area define decision rights, "tiebreaker," or a "veto power" process. This will aid the group when it reaches an impasse or becomes deadlocked on an issue.

The final area is accountability for tasks and projects. These are ground rules around record keeping, measurement of progress, accountability for commitments, timelines for completion, and consequences (positive and negative).

Each team member should understand and feel personally responsible for contributing to the ground rules, so it is best to take some time to "hash" out what a team's ground rules or operating principles are. All ideas should be considered. To illustrate, we have provided some examples of working ground rules from actual teams that we have worked with:

Engineering Team, Heavy Machine Manufacturing Company

- Fulfill every commitment and promise (do what you say you will do)
- Work hard, full effort, be totally committed
- Keep the "big picture in mind"
- Maintain a positive attitude
- Have confidence and believe in yourself
- Continually seek for improvement
- Be enthusiastic
- Cooperate, stay together, think win-win
- Put team goals ahead of personal goals
- Trust each other
- Be accountable, take ownership for your work/project
- Manage and control emotions

A Service Company

- Individual performance and group performance do not exclude each other
- Listen and learn to think outside of the box
- Be willing to take a personal risk
- Think before you act
- Have guts/courage
- Have fun
- Celebrate
- Be accountable
- Align

- Be honest

- Know the goal and concentrate on it

Sales Team for a Service Organization

- Unparalleled leadership, initiative, and empowerment

- Creativity and innovation

- Effective decision making

- Strategic thinking and well-calculated risks

- Management of details

- Solidifying processes and procedures

- Effective use of resources and managing costs

- Streamlining responsibilities

An organization that used the acronym CHARACTER

Competent
Hardworking
Accountable
Resourceful
Adroit
Caring
Thorough
Ethical
Respectful

CHAPTER
NINE

Environment:
Making Connections

9

Environment:
Making Connections

Introduction

In their natural habitat, clownfish are very vulnerable to their predators because of their bright color and poor ability to swim. They adapt to the situation by creating a mutual relationship with sea anemones, a marine polyp that resembles flowers but have tentacles. Clownfish are able to avoid the sting of an anemone, so the anemones provide a needed refuge and protection for the clownfish. In exchange, clownfish defend their host anemones. If young clownfish don't quickly find an anemone partner, they will not survive. Similarly, human teams can't survive without forming a strong, symbiotic partnership with key stakeholders, customers, sponsors, partners, and the resources of their environment.

In the late 1990s, a team of HR professionals from a medical products company invited us to facilitate some working sessions to help them find solutions to challenges they were facing. Interestingly enough, as we began the intervention, we found that their challenges and concerns were not rooted in the team itself, but rather in their relationships with other teams in the organization. Through this insightful experience, we discovered an interesting dynamic that teams confront, one rarely addressed in books on teamwork or in teamwork training; the nature of the environment in which the team exists has a significant impact on the team's effectiveness and its ultimate ability to reach peak performance.

Environment, the outer boarder of the Diamond Model of Teamwork, represents the world in which the team operates, more specifically it means people, teams, customers, stakeholders, and other entities that the team serves or is served by. We like to refer to them as the extended team because these alliances and connections influence team success. Everyone on the team needs to be concerned about building productive relationships with members in the environment, as working jointly, these teams form a virtual ecosystem of interdependencies and connections. Some of these ecosystem teams play a role either before or after a team is created. Each team needs to understand what it must accomplish, for whom, and when. Likewise, the other teams in the system must know what each team expects in order to create the synergies that are possible.

> The nature of the environment the team exists in has a significant impact on the team itself and its ultimate ability to reach peak performance.

The components of a team's environment (or extended team) can be internal or external to the organization. The relationships can be formal or informal. Extended teams generally comprise these groups:

- Organizational stakeholders

- Customers/clients

- Vendors/suppliers

- Functional peer teams or support groups (HR, IT. legal, safety, etc.)

In essence, the elements of the environment are those people and groups that a team needs in order to meet its promises to provide the products and services.

Benefits

Most teams are frequently disconnected from their environmental partners. In some cases, an enormous chasm separates teams and their extended team. But in studying and working with exceptional teams, we have found that they readily acknowledge the following benefits of establishing and fostering productive relationships with their important partners:

- Problems are identified early to the satisfaction of user groups.

- Members of the extended team are more prone to help, rather than criticize.

- Efforts are better coordinated and overlap and rework are reduced.

- Strategies are better executed.

- Alignment around organization-wide strategies increases.

- Support for cross-team projects and objectives is enhanced.

- Sharing of resources, information, and best practices increases.

You can begin to get a glimpse of what is possible if teams tap into the resources and expertise that are all around them.

Some opinion surveys done by R. Wells, described in *Tapping the Network Journal,* indicated that organizational issues like a lack of team training, unsupportive attitudes from upper management, and misaligned systems for rewarding performance were major factors contributing to team failure. Teams working in the same system can't work at cross purposes.

In countless hospitals around the world, patients can spend days being passed from one specialist to another. They are of-

ten given a variety of inconsistent diagnoses and have
to deal with wearisome treatment delays. But at the
Mayo Clinic, things are different: specialist teams work
together to determine diagnoses and treatment plans.
This integrated team approach has become an innovative way of treating patients. Cross-disciplinary teams have
broken down traditional barriers, interests, and turfs in order
to better serve the health care customer. Not every organization will benefit to the degree that the Mayo Clinic does from
its cross-team collaboration, but teams that can create a culture
and a team imperative that facilitates strong cross-team collaboration among extended team members can realize some
impressive gains.

Environment Close Up

While some relationships with extended teams may be very
complex and others simple, a very practical approach can be
applied to building and maintaining relationships, regardless
of complexity. Our research and field experience indicate that
a team can do five key things to develop strong and flexible
relationships with other entities that are crucial to its success.

1. Identification

The first key to effective external team relationships is obvious, yet significant, but most teams don't do it very well.
Team members should jointly identify the key groups or relationships that constitute their environment. To accomplish this,
the team should reflect on who they are accountable to. The
obvious answer will be stakeholders or customers, but that
thinking needs to be tested because the team may have some
less obvious accountabilities. Your team can dive a level deeper
in identifying the extended team by exploring the people and/
or groups that have a vested interest in the team. These overt
and hidden relationships may represent the people and groups

who provide guidance, direction, resources, regulations, support, tools, and other things that help the team function.

Once these relationships have been identified, the team needs to do a SWOT (Strengths, Weaknesses, Opportunities, Threats) analysis and collectively pinpoint potential relationship obstacles and opportunities. Just knowing who they are is not enough. The team needs to know how to interact with the other team or people and what could possibly go wrong so problems can be averted or addressed quickly. The old adage "knowledge is power" is very true here. Each team also needs to formulate a "contract," an agreement, or at least a tacit understanding of the needs and expectations of the extended teams.

2. Stakeholders Needs and Wants

To really know how to work well with others in the environment, all teams needs to know what the members of the environment want and need. Teams can get clarification about this by asking these questions:

- What are the deliverables our team is responsible for?

- What do our customers (internal and external) expect?

- Are we clear about what we need from our suppliers, and have we communicated it?

The needs and wants of stakeholders fall into two categories. One type is more tangible in nature. These "hard" wants and needs include things like: targets, quotas, specifications, requirements, time frames or due dates, formats, etc. They may even include legal, regulatory, and ethical requirements. The second type is more intangible in nature. These "softer" wants and needs include things such as communication, information, visibility, inclusion in the decision processes, motivation, confidentiality, involvement, creativity, etc.

We have a valued client who is the team leader of a functional area for a very large organization. His team provides and important service to the organization. We started working with this leader at a time when his team was disconnected with their environment and it started to impact the team's performance. They decided that to improve their ability to collaborate with other functional areas, they would need to benchmark their performance and get input directly from the environment.

The team figured that they best way to start the discovery process was to distribute a survey to the key members of their environment. Here are some of the questions they used to get a pulse on what was happening:

- Please rate our team's level of understanding of the needs and opportunities in your area of responsibility.

- Please rate our team's level of responsiveness to your area of responsibility.

- Please rate our team's frequency of communication with your area of responsibility.

- Please rate our team's ability to solve problems related to your area of responsibility.

- Please rate our team's level of contribution to the performance of your area of responsibility.

- Please rate your level of confidence in our team's ability to improve performance in your area of responsibility.

- Please rate out team's level of accountability to the organization's performance.

- Please rate the effectiveness of our team's processes.

They also requested written comments and suggestions for each of these areas. Using this approach, they quickly began to collect some important information about their team's impact on the environment. Some of the information was not a surprise, but they did learn some things that they had not recognized before. Making adjustments and applying the information to their team's direction, processes, and structure hasn't always been easy, they have committed to take it one step at a time and the people in the environment have appreciated that this team cares about their wants and needs.

Getting a handle on these types of wants and needs is crucial because these factors contribute to the level of trust that will exist across teams in the ecosystem. These factors will also open the door to a commitment to follow through and to accountability. Your team may also find it helpful to work directly with the group or people to identify, negotiate, and get clear on their needs and wants. This direct dialogue will leave no room for error or second guessing.

Ed Hoffman was the team leader of NASA's Academy of Program and Project Leadership. His approach to teamwork was described in the October 1999 issue of *Fast Company* magazine. Hoffman's immediate team comprised of contractors and consultants, relied on other NASA employees who provided support and instruction for academy students. During one particular class, the engineers who were participating in the course felt they were getting a textbook lecture and that it really didn't apply to their situations. The classroom became chaotic and people were frustrated. Ed learned that his internal customers were unhappy with the experience they were receiving and were planning to leave. He immediately dropped what he was doing and went to the classroom. Once in front of the group, he said, "Obviously, we're doing a lousy job of meeting your needs. What can we do to change that?" After a thorough and open discussion, Ed and his colleagues quickly fine tuned the workshop agenda and salvaged a success out of imminent disaster.

It takes courage and a vested interest in those being served to truly maximize your team's value to the organization. A team has to be clear about its value proposition and promise to the organization. Sometimes, you just have to ask your partners and engage in a candid, two-way communication. Later on, Ed got other NASA administrators involved, and guidelines and curriculum changed completely. Amazing synergy was created when Ed's team got clear about their customers' needs and wants.

> It takes courage and a vested interest in those being served to truly maximize your team's value to the organization.

3. Team Needs and Wants

On the flip side, teams need to, in good faith, share and contract for what they need and want from their extended team. The thing to remember is that the team's expectations and needed resources should not be born out of greed but rather out of the need to be effective. Teams must also address both project or task-related needs and wants, in addition to role and relationship needs. The lynchpin that will bring it all together, and the most crucial need to seek out, is operational feedback and information from the extended team to help the team know if it is reaching the targets and effectively serving those around it. Be authentic as you identify and communicate your teams' expectations and finally, work hard to keep your extended team in the loop so they can respond and adapt to the changing conditions of your team.

4. Connection and Communication

As is the case with almost every element of the Diamond Model of Teamwork, effective communication is at the heart of a productive extended team relationship. Solid communication between the team and members of the environment, including upper management, peer teams, and customers, fa-

cilitate unity, information sharing, conflict resolutions, and recognition. In the absence of clear, consistent, and reliable interactions the team and member of the environment will begin to
operate as two separate entities, and we all know what that
can lead to. The team itself will be asking for trouble if it can't
break down barriers and voluntarily open up dialogue, seek
assistance, and offer help. As our colleague and friend Dr. Richard Williams says: "Good communication leads to a greater
depth of understanding of intentions, empathy, and insights."
Once groups begin to understand each other, respect begins to
flourish and people value and appreciate each other. This, in
turn, leads to trust. Without trust no two groups can create the
synergy needed to accomplish ambitious goals.

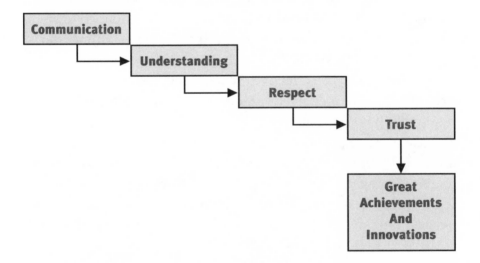

When the team is communicating effectively, the obvious
result will be enhanced coordination. We have also seen creative and breakthrough ideas surface and systems develop to
respond to problems and opportunities. Good communication
and coordination encourage sharing resources and working
together through challenges. With frequent connections between peer teams, conflict and competitiveness are less appar-

ent because trust is stronger and teams are positioned to provide assistance. Unfortunately, most connections between the team and the extended team occur when the team is doing exceptionally well or is failing. Yet a lot of synergy could be occurring at other times. To enhance connections, the team needs to identify how it will communicate with each member in the environment as each will have different approaches, needs, and frequencies, etc. A one-size-fits-all approach likely won't have positive outcomes for the team. Whatever information is communicated should be

- Accurate and clear

- Provided to the right people

- Provided in a constructive way.

Even taking this approach, the team should follow up on the communication to ensure the intended message has been accurately received.

One of our colleagues, James Gehrke, shared an example of the importance of communication with us. Several years ago, he had the opportunity to head up a new group within a company in the pharmaceutical industry. The objective of the group was to raise the effectiveness of the sales organization by focusing on management development for the sales managers. Up until that time there was no coordinated attempt to provide a standard approach to management development for the company worldwide. Working with sales organizations around the world, the team developed and rolled out a curriculum designed to meet the basic needs of first line managers in the sales force.

Soon, other departments in the countries began requesting the same programs. It wasn't long until James' team was delivering programs to all managers, both sales and non-sales. While the markets were happy about the support they were receiving, James discovered that not everyone was happy. In each region around the world, Human Resources had assigned a colleague to look after talent planning. His team began to receive feedback that they were seen as competing with this HR talent management initiative.

In the beginning, the team was not even aware that this other HR team existed because James' team was content with maximizing the number of satisfied internal customers they could generate. The HR team insisted that they should be the only team providing training to those groups outside of the field force, since they had the task with providing development for non-sales groups. This caused resistance from the markets, since the HR team could not provide the amount of training that James' team was providing in various languages around the world. It wasn't long until fighting and arguing increased between the two teams. Each tried to persuade their market customers that their team was best positioned to provide the needed training. Eventually it negatively affected the way both teams were perceived and the ability to effectively meet the customer's needs.

Overtime, both teams realized that they needed to project a united front to the internal customers. The most important objective was to raise organizational performance, and not who got the most credit for providing it. They began to meet as cross-functional teams to identify the problems facing the customers and to brainstorm the best way to resolve them. Soon, both James' team and the HR team were able to produce a common approach to leadership development. Then a resource guide that identified all of the global development resources was jointly developed, published, and distributed. This of course was a benefit to the customers, but it also was great for the teams. Both the HR and James' team had developed excellent tools and they realized that they needed each other. Rather than competing against each other, there was more to gain by working together.

If they had not opened up the lines of communication, they never would have come to this understanding and respect for one another. Working together over time, they learned they could trust each other. The biggest winners were our customers, because they received better products than either team could deliver alone.

John Miller, in his book QBQ, sums it up, "... our organizations can be places where instead of finger-pointing, procrastinating, and 'we-theying' ourselves into the ground, we bring out the best in each other, work together the way teams are supposed to and make great things happen."

5. Adaptation

In organizations fraught with change or saddled with targets that are continually moving, teams have to be able to adapt to the changing conditions in their environment. Teams can choose to be flexible or can make things difficult by sticking to their guns and insisting on the status quo. There is no sure-fire answer for making a team flexible. But, it starts with the fundamental culture of the team and an expectation that team members themselves are adaptable. The team can do a lot in this area just by knowing that change is coming and then regularly opening up dialogue about what the team needs to do to respond to its extended team. The team's energy needs to be directed away from politics and towards achieving results. Great synergy emerges when teams and people can work across borders and combine their efforts to create new value.

Pine trees have an interesting way of adapting to their environment. If a pine tree is growing on a steep surface and the hill starts to erode or slide, the tree's trunk will begin to bend so that the tree continues to grow upward towards the sun, instead of at an angle. So should be the case with teams. Effective teams first learn the environment in which they function and how it contributes to the team's success. Then as situations, needs, requirements, and other factors change around them, they can adapt while still maintaining their focus on the direction and purpose they have set forth.

In conclusion, the success of the relationships between the team and the environment is largely within the team's control. But, despite the best of intentions, a team's ability to create important links is helped or hindered by the nature of the organization. We find that these team-to-team relationships thrive when organizations support their efforts in these ways:

- The organization has a clear vision and purpose that teams align themselves with.

- The organization sustains and nurtures programs and initiatives.

- Teams are empowered to be innovative and to take calculated risks.

- The organization doesn't always expect teams to conform to the status quo and long-term traditions.

- Rumors and secrets do not flow through the organization.

- When teams create innovative solutions or think outside of the box they are not overruled too often.

- The organization encourages teams to benchmark and compare their operations with those of other teams and organizations.

- Teams are not micromanaged by upper management.

- Teams are included in important decisions.

- A balanced amount of change is introduced.

If your team finds itself in a less-than-ideal situation, it will just have to do its best to influence the organization in a positive way.

In Summary

With any relationship a team has, there are two potential outcomes. One outcome is a relationship marred by

- Tensions and conflict
- Misunderstandings
- Inefficiency
- Disappointment
- Resistance
- Complications

Or a team can bridge the chasm, and the outcome in this case is

- Lasting solutions
- Trust and mutual respect
- Creativity and innovation
- Commitment
- Satisfaction
- And, of course, results!

The job facing teams is deciding which outcome is preferred as they work with the strategic partners in their environment.

Environment is the final piece of the Diamond Model of Teamwork. Teams that are able to incorporate the facets of the diamond into their work will create lasting results and be better positioned to face the challenges and obstacles that will inevitably come their way. It will not always be perfect, but we believe and have witnessed that the best teams are able to get a handle on these forces in their team and reach new levels of success.

CHAPTER
TEN

Senior Leadership Teams

10

Senior Leadership Teams

From time to time we get asked why we spend a lot of our time helping senior leadership teams achieve a high level of performance and cohesiveness. For us the answer is simple. Management teams are in the spotlight. Everyone takes behavioral cues from the leadership team-not to mention that the effectiveness and outcomes of a leadership team reverberate throughout the entire organization. If the senior team isn't highly functional, how can the organization as a whole ever have a chance at being successful in building wealth for investors, delivering customer value, and creating security for workers? When it comes right down to it, management teams have a responsibility to establish long-range strategy and direction, and the buck stops with them for results. The final reason why senior leadership teams have to gel is because senior leaders juggle many critical priorities at the same time. Without some close coordination and support, it can cause serious burnout and have substantial impact on results.

In some ways, senior leadership teams aren't much different from any team that is trying to work together for the best interest of the group and trying to sustain the business and their own livelihoods. These teams remind us of gardening. Most people have tried to grow something like a beautiful rose, some tender tulips, herbs, or a favorite vegetable. Af-

ter the planting, watering, fertilizing, and sunlight, you notice that other things begin to take advantage of the fertile condition you have created...weeds—the pesky kind. It seems that no matter how hard you work on pulling, they inevitably return. You might try to pull them out but only get half the root, allowing them to spring up again. Or perhaps the wind blows some new seeds in and a fresh crop of weeds emerges. Senior leadership teams are like gardens, but instead of weeds they have issues. These issues crop up all the time in the course of doing business and can rob teams of the critical ingredients for success, as well as suck all the joy out of seeing a business grow and flourish. Issues are normal and natural; just like weeds in a garden, they are part of the process. In teams, the goal is not to eradicate issues forever, because that's impossible. Rather, teamwork for leadership teams requires learning the process of channeling these issues in productive directions so that they are not a distraction, a drain on energy, or a source of frustration. The litmus test of high-performance teams at any level is the ability and confidence of the team to solve the usual and unusual problems that crop up and then learn from them for the future. But learning how to do this is an art that requires

The litmus test of high-performance teams at any level is the ability and confidence of the team to solve the usual and unusual problems that crop up and then learn from them for the future.

discipline for senior leadership teams—for any team for that matter. We just finished working with an IT leadership team that has responsibility for all of North and South America. At the end of their first three-day intensive meeting, 139 issues had been identified as a result of years of misalignment and miscommunication. They will have to tackle these challenges in a productive way so they can get back on track and enhance their value to the organization.

This chapter explores some of the special challenges lead-

 ership teams face and what they need to focus on to make their own special contribution to the business. Clearly, when a collection of people assemble, who are hard charging, very smart, and have some big egos and a bit of power and authority, the mix can be very volatile. Teamwork is usually the last thing on their minds. In fact, some people think that team development is nothing more than a bunch of wimpy people hugging trees, singing kumbaya, and staring at a flame. That's what they think until they are sitting in a boat on a tricky river where they all have to row in the same direction in order to navigate a nasty rapid, or ascend a peak that requires more cooperation than they have ever experienced in their life, spending a day walking the Gettysburg Battlefields and feeling the strategic decisions that cost 50,000 casualties but became the turning point of the Civil War, or experiencing the Holocaust Museum and seeing the tragic results of misused power.

We have seen many teams get "vapor locked" from these special challenges and issues over the past 30 years as we have designed, conducted, and facilitated leadership team retreats, meetings, and conferences aimed at helping management teams rise to the next level of performance and cohesiveness. While we could devote another book to the topic, we will explore some of the major dysfunctions any senior leadership team needs to confront to get on the path to greatness.

1. "Are we better together?"

This is the question one business leader asked of his team, a team responsible for a multibillion dollar operation. Within his span of control sat four division leaders and the usual cast of supporting team members from legal, human resources, IT, sales and marketing, and countless other areas. Making a pact to truly share responsibility for the whole business is the real issue here. It is a given that each member of this senior team is fiercely competitive, independent, and strong-willed. Intense people tend to rise to the top, and as we said earlier in the book, they are high-performing individuals who haven't necessarily been trained or conditioned to work as a high-performing unit. It is an extreme challenge to get these individuals to think holistically, to consider the performance of the entire organization, not just the performance of their business units, divisions, or functional areas.

Over the years, this team had adopted the notion that their individual responsibilities and contributions to the team ended when they achieved the goals required of their own functional area. They simply did not see themselves as members of a "leadership team" jointly responsible for steering the company and for helping others who might be facing a special challenge. Don't get us wrong; during our interviews and on surveys, this group was always willing to step up if they had a problem with another team member. They were even pretty good in a crisis, such as when there was a regularatory issue, a competitive threat, or when a fire ripped through a key facility within one of the business units. It was, in fact, when things were pretty normal that the team lost horsepower. This team suffered from a failure to be more proactive, strategic, and innovative. It was also unable to work together on developing talent, optimizing customer relationships, and cross selling. In short, an inability to find synergy across the silos plagues many teams. But further complicating the challenge of working together was the incentive system. It was a classic situation where individuals received bonuses based on their own personal goals and unit profit and loss statements, rather than the combined organizational results. It certainly wasn't a broken team. In fact, the individual effort, intelligence, and perseverance of each member would not allow them to fail as individuals. If members wanted

> **"A single arrow is easily broken, but not ten in a bundle."**
> – *Japanese Saying*

to take a narrow view of the situation, they could easily ask the "why" questions. Why should I spend time and energy? Why should I share resources and knowledge? Why should I expose myself to feedback, suggestions, and sensitivity from other leaders when I could lay low, take care of my own business, and watch the feeding frenzy unfold when another leader is in trouble? But, if members of a leadership team can resolve their questions, they will create a solid footing on which the team can grow and produce value for all stakeholders.

2. "Who are you anyway?"

This question really hit home one day when we explored it during a two-day offsite workshop involving a management team we had been working with on a trimester basis for nearly five years. We had met face-to-face with this team for more than 12 sessions. They had come a long way and experienced many productive and memorable times together. We were at a loss as to what type of experience would serve them the most, then we came up with a brilliant idea: we asked them! We asked them for the focal point or key objective for the next session and we were shocked at the result. They said that they simply wanted to get to know each other better and create a foundation of trust. Our jaws dropped because after all the high-impact exercises, events, and experiences we had facilitated in previous sessions, we just hadn't expected this, especially since all of them worked next door to each other in a suite of offices that spanned an area of about 600 square feet around a reception area where they shared two assistants. They probably saw each other multiple times every day. They attended meetings together and sometimes traveled to the field together. As

> "The man who gets the most satisfactory results is not always the man with the brilliant single mind, but rather the man who can best coordinate the brains and talents of his associates."
>
> – *W. Alton Jones*

we dug further, we learned that all this business activity was very superficial and that they really didn't know what made each other tick, what their dreams and aspirations were, what they needed from the team, and what drove them away from wanting to collaborate. It began to make perfect sense. Here was a group of perfectly normal adults who worked around each other all the time. Yet they didn't really understand each other's styles, motives, rationale, thought processes, and life experiences that molded who they are today. So we didn't go anywhere exotic, but simply found some quiet meeting space. In fact, it was at the home of the person who founded the company 75 years earlier, a home that had been carefully preserved by the family on a nice, but not opulent, 10-acre estate that was used from time to time for board meetings, family outings, and even company picnics. It was quiet, relaxed, and slightly off the beaten path. We spent the first morning doing the usual strategic review, and then we set the heavy business discussion aside and made the deep dive into who they are, where they came from, what they stand for, what drives them, and what alienates them. It was a tough group, but they melted fast as they opened up and moved into this process of disclosure. After we set it up and demonstrated how the sharing would work, the CEO, Dave, volunteered to go first. He set the tone, and the true openness that was created has served them well during future discussions about critical issues like mergers, acquisitions, land consolidations, and where to deploy capital. After the experience, they listened to each other better, they understood each other's point of view, they kept an open mind, and they became comfortable giving each other feedback or advice about the business. It was an incredible capstone to an exciting series of sessions that we were honored to guide and assist.

3. "May I share some feedback?"

This is a classic question. It is even a little hard to under-

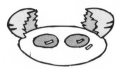 stand, at times, considering the type of people who join a management team. Giving each other feedback would be easy, but a tender veil separates people and they are reluctant to step through it. Or people feel that if they share their feelings about other team members, the flood gates of criticism will be open. So many executives and leaders walk on eggshells and tiptoe around each other. They create these unspoken agreements: if you don't criticize me, I won't criticize you.

The other dynamic that occurs is just the opposite, that is, those members who brutally attack team members in front of others. They sometimes seem to derive a sadistic joy from exposing the travails of others in public. What's more, they easily become defensive and don't listen to or process the opinions or perceptions of others. They may have a good point, but they tear people apart in an effort to elevate themselves at the expense of others.

There has to be a middle ground, where team members will step up courageously and tell the emperor (or anyone for that matter) if he has no clothes on. But it has to be done with skill, at the right time, in the right place, and with the right intentions. We use a technique called the "APB" Exercise (Alternate Possible Behavior) during our senior-leadership team development meetings to get the process started. It is a balanced way for executives and senior leaders to begin sharing feedback of all kinds (both positive and negative). At first it is anonymous and written. Later it is verbal and spontaneous. Pretty soon executive teams we work with really start to like the process. One high-performing team, that we referred to earlier, is the Navy's Blue Angels. They understand the value of candid and fair feedback. After every show

> "Nothing else can quite substitute for a few well-chosen, well-timed, sincere words of praise. They're absolutely free—and worth a fortune."
>
> *– Sam Walton*
> *Founder of Walmart*

they do an exhaustive debrief of their performance. They discuss the highs and lows, the safety issues, and the cosmetics or profile of the flight. It is a ritual. When members of the team discuss or expose a flaw in someone's effort, that team member explains that he/she will take accountability, fix the mistakes, and ritually say, "I am glad to be here." They know it is an honor to be on this elite team that represents the whole fleet. They also acknowledge they are humans, they make mistakes, and they need to take corrective actions on a routine basis. But it's okay! Everyone has his/her turn to get feedback. In fact, it is an honor because it only makes the team stronger. So it is with any leadership team. There needs to be a steady flow of well-intentioned constructive feedback.

4. "Is there a dead moose in the room?"

This dysfunction is a close relative of the third dysfunction in the sense that it speaks to the whole issue of communication. Senior leadership teams often maintain a conspiracy of silence when it comes to important and sensitive issues. Some executives play it too close to the vest, lacking the courage needed to say what they think. Some people refer to this phenomena as "group think." As we mentioned earlier in the book, Jerry Harvey refers to it as the "Abilene Paradox": a group's inability to raise deep underlying questions, concerns, and reservations about a course of action. It is a form of collusion that is vicious and insidious. Avoiding this dysfunction requires a team that is willing to take risks, members who are in touch with their own emotional intelligence, and who feel secure enough in the group to be honest with each other. We like to call this "peel-

> "A highly effective, highly cohesive team is a transitory state in a dynamic process. Business management will improve significantly when executives respect the values of that process and work with its dynamics."
>
> – *Edwin Lee*

ing" the onion—not allowing the group to stay at the surface when it needs to uncover serious, underlying questions and issues about the business or, even more importantly, about the trust level or relationship. In some cases, the biggest issue with a senior team is "calling out the dead moose" when the issues pertain specifically to something the CEO or the COO is proposing. Here are some examples:

- The senior leader's apparent preference for a pet project

- Fear of the senior leader's power and authority when budgets are being discussed

- Assumptions that everyone is on board with a controversial strategy

- Fear of being alienated or appearing insubordinate to the senior leader for voicing contrarian views

- Inability to confront awkward or sensitive issues like someone's miscalculations, low performance, or poor treatment of people

- Unwillingness to take collective ownership required to resolve a difficult problem

In the beginning, a skilled facilitator may be needed to show a team how to "smoke out" these fears, lingering doubts, and unresolved problems. It is the Knowing vs. Doing Gap that groups have to be trained and coached to detect. That is, they know that the smelly moose is in the room, but something is blocking a proper discussion and resolution. If "the moose" isn't handled, it will inevitably come back with a vengeance in the form of finger pointing and blame in a key meetings, discussions around the water cooler, or in the break room. An undercurrent builds as people grumble and express their dissatisfaction behind the back of the very person who needs to hear it the most.

We have seen it in so many leadership teams: members walk out the door nodding their heads in agreement, but the lack of action, enthusiasm, and commitment indicates that it was a false consensus—one of the worst things a team can do to itself, to its leaders, and to the organization as a whole. If teams don't become comfortable discussing the undiscussable, raising sensitive issues, or surfacing disagreements and concerns, they will lose a lot of creativity, trust, and unity. Furthermore, the whole organization will see and mimic this behavior.

> "Great teamwork is the only way we create the breakthroughs that define our careers."
> – *Pat Riley*

One group we enjoy working with closely has adopted the ground rule: "Discuss, Decide, and Champion" to eliminate the Knowing vs. Doing Gap or to signal the need for more debate, discussion, and argument if someone is not ready to support the consensus that is being forged. This is the time for team members to be less political and manipulative if they are not feeling connected to the decision or have hunches and questions that need to be explored.

This full disclosure can be a hard thing for many groups to achieve. Another one of our clients likes to call it "getting naked around the issues." It may be an odd choice of words, but it works for him and everyone knows that this is the opportunity to honestly share thoughts. Breaking the willing or unwilling conspiracy of silence requires ground rules and expectations about how members will behave in discussions. These rules need to be defined, taken serious, referred to, and enforced by everyone as the team moves into deeper emotional waters and more complex and crucial conversations.

5. "Whom do you trust?"

Trust is a cornerstone for any team. Members cannot hope for better strategies, more consistent performance, or a more positive work experience if a foundation of trust is missing. There is no shortcut when it comes to building trust. It takes time, is very fragile, and can erode quickly with a few missteps. Some members of senior teams we work with have two very contrasting positions on trusting their colleagues. One type of person is willing to give others the benefit of the doubt from the beginning. They take as a given, that people are to be trusted until proven otherwise. The other type of person believes that trust has to be earned, as well as demonstrated with words and actions. They won't trust you until you have proven that you are trustworthy. So trust becomes a crucial ingredient for senior teams, but it can be complicated. In its simplest form, trust centers on intentions. When you have the best intentions of the other party in mind, you are doing what you need to do to be trustworthy. If you look deeper you will see that trust is composed of six ingredients. Senior team members have to be effective in these six areas if trust is going to grow and flourish:

> "In the end, all business operations can be reduced to three words: people, product and profits. Unless you've got a good team, you can't do much with the other two."
>
> *– Lee Iacocca*

a) Consistency

Trust in a leadership team will be very uneven if one or more members don't consistently deliver the results and performance that the team needs. If people are coming up short, others on the team will fear that they will be held responsible for the shortfall. In essence, team members have to have a track record that indicates that they step up and deliver; if not, the whole team will be nervous and hesitant to trust each other.

b) Competence

Senior-leadership team members must believe that their

colleagues have the intellectual capacity to conquer complex problems, navigate strategies, and make quality decisions. Members of leadership teams need the credentials, experience, and competencies. They have to know what they are talking about and doing without question. Amazingly, a recent study showed that 80% of senior managers believe they possess the necessary skills to fulfill their roles, but when asked if their colleagues did, only 30% said yes.

c) Character

The next element of trust is character. The members of the team need to ascribe to a set of common values and beliefs. They have to work in a way that is aligned with common values. Each team needs to define what character traits and qualities are most important to their success. It might include integrity, loyalty, involvement, collaboration, etc. When the actions of its members align with these core beliefs, team members gain trust and respect.

> **"Excellence is not an accomplishment. It is a spirit, a never-ending process."**
> – *Lawrence M. Miller*

d) Communication

If the team lacks open communication, trust will suffer. Because the six dysfunctions are closely interconnected, one dysfunction can ignite and spread to other dysfunctions. In this case, if the interactions are not open or if hidden agendas, games, and strategies preclude honest communication, trust will quickly fizzle out.

e) Change

Trust tends to develop when people are adaptable, rather than stubbornly stuck in old ways of thinking and acting. If people on the team are unwilling to cooperate, compromise, and experiment, deep divisions result. Jack Gibb, now retired from Stanford University, wrote an article on the causes of defensiveness and mistrust in groups and found that when people are set in their ways, "certain" as he calls it, others are repelled and driven away. If others feel there is no hope of contributing ideas, shaping decisions, or bringing about change, there is no way to build a trusting relationship.

f) Caring

People have to know that their fellow team members see the big picture and care about it as much as or even more than their own self-interest. A trusting team accepts the fact that individuals must be willing to sacrifice and endure personal pain in some situations if their actions will benefit the long-term interests of the organization. If there is too much greed or self-centeredness, people begin to pursue a policy of self-protection, manipulating and plotting ways to maximize their personal gains. Everyone becomes too competitive with each other and trust goes out the window.

According to a study by McKinsey and Company, 65% of respondents in their top-team database indicate that trust is a real issue for their teams. The battle for trust is never over, and it has to be an open discussion item during leadership-team retreats.

Senior leadership teams don't magically coalesce overnight. They don't become high-performing teams because their offices are close to each other. And really bright people do not always naturally form a team. Nor do people who have risen to high levels in an organization always have special insights or talents to become a team. In fact, it could be just the opposite. All of these factors help explain why teams at the top really struggle to achieve their full potential. In fact, in the McKinsey study mentioned earlier, only 20% of executives surveyed thought their team was a high-performing one. Yet we know from our own practice that with a little investment, some skilled facilitation, and a desire by senior members, you can change teams at the top, you can make the process of team discovery and learning explicit, and you can rapidly achieve significant results that will endure with sustained efforts.

"Only 20% of executives surveyed thought their team was a high performing one."
– McKinsey and Company

We have seen a variety of leadership teams learn how to become both challenging and supportive, and how to honestly assess their own performance, explore successes and failures objectively, and benchmark organizations outside of their own industry to discovery new ways of tackling challenges. Finally, we have witnessed teams reflect deeply on the causes of problems and identify areas where they can add the most value to the organization. In the end, these teams have created better strategies, performed more consistently, discovered areas for synergy, and gained the confidence of investors and stakeholders. One newly formed leadership team that we worked with wisely identified and successfully worked through eight critical questions before they began any substantive problem solving or decision making. The critical questions were:

1. What value can this team produce by working together more closely?

2. What space or area of responsibility is the domain of this team?

3. Why does the team exists?

4. What is the role and authority of the team's leader?

5. What kind of decision making process or style will we adopt?

6. What are the ground rules for meetings and behavioral expectations of our members (how will we play together)?

7. What do we need to do to get to know each other better?

8. What do we need to do to bridge the gap between the operational business leaders and staff or functional leaders?

You might have noticed that this is a lot of "We" and not a lot of "It". For senior teams, it is premature to tackle the "It" until the team comes together.

"A study at Cornell University's Johnson Graduate School of Management found that compassion and building teamwork will be two of the most important characteristics business leaders will need for success a decade from now."

– Doc Childre and Bruce Cryer

As investor expectations keep rising, top teams cannot wait years to improve their performance. Senior teams must accelerate the pace of change in order to avoid losing the confidence of key constituents. Any business needs a flow of money, capital, goods, services, and resources to succeed. Also as part of the mix, an organization depends on a flow of information, ideas, solutions, and decisions, especially within the leadership team. It isn't going to be enough to stand up to global competition and the usual business threats, or for a few individual leaders to create a good profit and loss statement in isolation from colleagues and other business units. Organizations can no longer operate as a collection of isolated silos that don't share information, ideas, and resources. Senior teams must step up and be the example for the rest of the organization to follow.

CHAPTER
ELEVEN

Conclusion

11

Conclusion

Our corporate office is located near the site of the 2002 Olympic Winter Games, so we had the opportunity to immerse ourselves in the electrifying Olympic experience. During the two-and-a-half week sports celebration, we discovered that one of the most fascinating team sports in the winter games is the bobsled competition. Bobsled teams comprise two or four athletes who jump into a "bob" and speed down an icy run, typically about 1500 meters long. If you have ever driven on an icy road, you have an inkling of what it might be like, except the bobsled is traveling at an explosive 135 kilometers per hour (~84 miles per hour). Since the principles of teamwork are very universal, there are some fascinating parallels that can be drawn between bobsled teams and the Diamond Model of Teamwork.

One of the most important elements of a good bobsled run is a great start. A fast start is necessary so the sled has enough momentum to power it through the run and successfully compete, just as a team needs a shared and clearly defined Direction. Synchronized effort and sprinting of all the team members is required to get the bobsled, which can weigh hundreds of pounds, from a complete stop to lightning-fast speed. Even if the driver has an ideal line, a great start still requires a focused effort by everyone involved. Similar to a team's direction, the run is not a straight shot. Sledders may have to navigate through 15 or 20 turns in a run.

Each bobsled team member has specific roles and subtle responsibilities, resembling the Structure of a high-performance team. The team has a driver (Leader) in the front, a brakeman in the rear, and the "push athletes" or middle sledders. The middle sledders do most of the work at the start, and while their additional weight and ability to lean in the right direction at the proper moment increase the speed of the sled, the additional weight can also make it more difficult to steer. Nevertheless, they still play a critical role in the team reaching its final objective—being the fastest sled.

A bobsled team must also adhere to the many rules, regulations, and processes that are set in place by Olympic officials, just as any high-performing team is clear about its processes and the regulations it has to operate under. When a bobsled completes a run, the team may be checked for weight and sled specifications by the officials. Additionally, officials may verify that the sled runners have not been coated with silicone or illegally warmed up to increase speed.

The best teams in business are made up of talented and committed team members; this is also the case in bobsledding. The sport went through substantial changes in the early fifties, which had a direct impact on sledders. Up to that point, sledders typically had heavy body weights so the sled could gather more speed. But when weight limits were instituted, sledders had to become leaner and meaner, so they engaged in ongoing conditioning to stay in top form. This additional effort enabled them to maintain the strength and coordination needed to keep the sled in the best line throughout the run. But now, it takes more than just a conditioned body. Team members also need courage and an excellent sense of balance to help keep the sled in a perfect racing line. Precise move-

> The best teams in business are made up of talented and committed team members; this is also the case in bobsledding.

ment is required by the crew as the driver steers the team toward success.

Just like a good bobsled team, high-performance business teams don't happen by accident or luck. They require initial dues and occasional discomforts, dedicated efforts, a willingness to experiment a little, and persistence to master the skills needed to achieve their goals. Healthy productive teams are good for business. Good teams and good team players are essential to future success. We can't envision a scenario, where society, business organizations, or any other type of organization won't need teamwork. It's an arduous journey of continuous learning, trial and error, and illusive perfection. But if a team uses the elements and tools in the Diamond Model of Teamwork as a framework, performance, cohesion, and synergy will be enhanced and the team will be well on its way to new levels of productivity and success. A bobsled team doesn't get to the Olympics by getting the latest technology in sleds, aerodynamic helmets, or scientifically designed fabrics for their uniforms. All of this helps but will be of little value if you can't create the communication, passion, and cohesiveness required for the team to work in unison. Be ready for an exhilarating ride because once you get things started, the chemistry kicks in, and the elements begin to take hold, your team will be on the fast track to success.

Take your time as you get started. You don't have to perfect every aspect of your team overnight. Just start applying some of these ideas where they will make the greatest impact and create a firm foundation for results to begin to emerge.

As we said in the beginning, there really is no secret and no magic is involved; the team approach can be introduced and executed by any team with the desire to do it! Good luck in your journey.

Appendix

The Exploring Teamwork Workshop from CMOE

Workshop Overview

There are many types of work groups and teams that exist in organizations. Few, however, function at peak levels. Because effective teamwork can be challenging to achieve, CMOE's Exploring Teamwork Workshop assists teams with core issues such as improving communication, tapping into creativity, maximizing resources, overcoming resistance, dealing with change in a positive way, and increasing productivity.

Exploring Teamwork is a powerful, experience-based workshop that shows participants how to build and sustain a high performance team, as well as how to develop teamwork skills at the individual level. The experiential nature of the training, combined with adult learning methods, ensures an exciting and memorable event. Participants walk away with an integrated set of skills, knowledge, and plans to renew team spirit, enhance performance, and improve team leadership. When these skills are applied, teams are stronger, more productive, and more aligned in purpose than ever before.

The Exploring Teamwork Workshop is tailored for intact teams, cross-functional teams, or a mixed group of individuals. The workshop is customized to each organization's specific team issues and needs.

Workshop Objectives

Participants will:

- Have an exciting learning experience that will raise their level of interest in and commitment to teamwork.

- Discover new methods to enhance team effectiveness and produce creative solutions to team challenges.

- Explore ways to build team motivation and revitalize commitment.

- Discover tools and resources that can be used to instill team cohesiveness.

- Gain personal insight about individual actions and behaviors that add to or detract from teamwork.

- Understand the:

  - Role and value of team leadership in achieving results.

  - Necessity of effective personal and interpersonal communication.

  - Ways to utilize the resources and talents within the team.

  - Importance of goals and vision.

  - Methods of problem-solving and of handling conflict and differences.

Workshop Outline

- Introduction and Orientation to "Exploring Teamwork"

- The Meaning of and Business Case for a High-Performance team

- Exercise—The Need for Teamwork and General Principles about Team Dysfunction

- Core Team Values

- Team Project/Exercise

- Critical Teamwork Issues and Discussion Topics

- The Teamwork Model In-Depth (the path to success)

- Exercise—the Value of Cross-Teaming, Communication, and Team Member Contribution to the Group Effort

- The Exploring Teamwork Assessment (assess the overall team health)

- Team Tools, Resources, and Processes

- Practical Solutions to Real Team Issues and Challenges

- Action Plans

Workshop Design

The Exploring Teamwork Workshop can be delivered in a one, two, or three day format at a location of your choice. CMOE also offers its retreat lodge, "Moose Meadows LLC," nestled in the mountains just 45 minutes from Salt Lake International Airport. It provides teams with a comfortable environment in a remote location and accommodates up to 16 people for one to three days and nights. Moose Meadows is the ideal location for intact, executive, and leadership teams to focus on critical tasks though a wide range of indoor and outdoor experiential activities and learning opportunities.

For more information about the Exploring Teamwork Workshop or other CMOE Workshops and Services, please call (801) 569-3444 or visit www.cmoe.com.

High Adventure Team Retreats
From CMOE

Retreat Overview

For organizations who want to take their teams to new heights, CMOE offers High Adventure Team Retreats. These retreats are designed to expand participants' comfort zones to overcome fears and barriers that prevent teams from reaching their fullest potential. Once teams are able to overcome team challenges and develop necessary team skills, business results will follow.

Team retreats are effective solutions for:

- Enhancing team cohesion
- Improving team problem solving
- Unleashing team potential
- Infusing energy and excitement
- Other critical team behaviors

Retreat Design

CMOE's High Adventure Team Retreats are typically 3-5 day events. Utilizing sites worldwide, we offer a variety of retreat settings, including the raging rapids of the Colorado River, the scenic red rocks of the Utah/Arizona border, the beautiful backwoods of the Sawtooth Mountain Range in Idaho, and others.

For more information about High Adventure Team Retreats or other CMOE Workshops and Services, please call (801)569-3444 or visit www.cmoe.com.

Senior Leadership Team Development from CMOE

Leadership Team Development Overview

A functional leadership team is at the heart of every successful organization. Unfortunately, building a cohesive leadership team can be difficult, at best, because of conflict, time pressures, egos, withholding information, and isolation at the senior level. However, it is vital to support these leaders and their teams by providing opportunities to continually develop and maintain a high level of performance. CMOE offers custom designed leadership team development solutions that enable leaders to set direction and build teams so members are aligned, supportive, and informed. These development events are customized around critical business issues such as:

- Organizational strategy
- Business planning
- Leading change
- Conflict and resolution
- Alignment across functions
- Organizational culture
- Merger and acquisition integration
- Leadership skill development
- Problem solving
- Talent management

- Newly formed teams

- Organizational growth

- Information exchange

- Innovation

Leadership Team Development Design

CMOE's Senior Leadership Team Development solutions are a great opportunity for leadership teams to call a "time out" to reconnect, reenergize, and realign. The events or retreats are designed and delivered in a way that addresses the unique and sometimes complex needs of leadership teams. Events and retreats are led by highly experienced facilitators who help leadership teams get out of their comfort zone to explore key issues and pre-selected "areas for change" as well as build new levels of cohesiveness, communication, innovation, trust, and growth for the team. They can be held off-site utilizing our recommended retreat locations world-wide or held near the office for an experience that is close by, but a world away.

For more information about Senior Leadership Team Development or other CMOE Workshops and Services, please call (801)569-3444 or visit www.cmoe.com.

Other books from CMOE Press

The Coach: Creating Partnerships for a Competitive Edge

Win-Win Partnerships: Be on the Leading Edge with Synergistic Coaching

Leading Groups to Solutions: A Practical Guide for Facilitators and Team Members

Ahead of the Curve: A Guide to Applied Strategic Thinking

Teamwork: We Have Met the Enemy and They are Us

To order call (801)569-3444 or visit www.cmoe.com.